The Three Causes of War

The path to abolish all of the warlike conflicts

Cacildo Marques

ISBN: **978-1711765686**

Cover design: French soldiers training shot - 1916
(time.com)

Episteme Ed

Marques, Cacildo
The three causes of war: The path to abolish all of the warlike
conflicts/ Cacildo Marques. Maryland, 2019.

146p.

ISBN: **978-1711765686**

1. War. 2. Causes of War. I. Title   DDC 355.027

The Three Causes of War

Cacildo Marques

CONTENTS

Preface

We only knew the motivations

Many academic works have sought to decipher the "causes of war". The title appears in this way, "Causes of War", in books and articles. But, as this book says, it is necessary to distinguish between causes and motivations. Even Clausewitz imagines presenting causes, understood as political objectives, which is limited, in fact, within the scope of the motivations for war. Until the beginning of the 21st century, studies on motivations brought a wealth of analysis, while those that deal with causes had only been tangential to the facts.

The motivations, which many scholars consider to be causes, account for:

1) Territorial gain;
2) Economic gain;
3) Religious differences;
4) Revenge;
5) Defense of nationalism.

Some wars mix two or more of these motivations. As for dimensions, warlike conflicts can be (a) international war; (b) civil war; or (c) revolutionary war, or guerrilla war. There are authors who confuse these three dimensions with motivations.

The causes, as we shall see in the text, are biological, and manifest in society as phenomena of Psychology, since war is realized as a behavioral result.

After World War II, intuition, not to be confused with mere guessing, brought to the great administrators and scholars less susceptible to partisan bias the realization that dictators with lifelong pretensions, with Hitler as the most blatant example, lead to the board of the struggles between peoples a force that goes beyond the mere territory of motivation.

From there we departed to develop the set of conceptual tools that led to the capture of the three causes, which are shown and discussed in this book.

Cacildo Marques, Nov 2019.

The Three Causes of War

Chapter 1 - Worldwide

We live, in the first decades of the 21ˢᵗ century, am era when, for the first time in history, we can see the abolition of all war in the world.

This happens for two reasons: Firstly, we have made great progress in the organizing among peoples, especially the UN, founded in 1945, with the main objective of promoting peace among the various countries of the world; secondly, we can already consider that we have diagnosed the root cause of war conflicts.

There are three war-gene11rating factors, which make up what was called the "tripod of the historical tragedy" in the book *The Brussels Crisis* (2012). And there are three levels of war, considering its scope and its actors. The largest one is the international war, waged by one or more countries against another country, or other countries. The second level is the civil war, which occurs when a country is divided in two or more fighting factions, often with division of territories. The third, and smaller, is the guerrilla war, which is a war promoted not by one country or group of countries, nor by a large part of one country against another, in what constitutes a civil war, but by a a political or religious group that, in an organized manner, under internally recognized leadership, confronts the army or police forces of the country in which it is installed, and may, depending on its progress in the trenches, even demand that the country's established government be aided by forces from other countries.

A group that acts as a guerrilla, but is only a band of delinquents, without a political partisan or religious characterization, should not be understood as a faction waging war, because this is a case to be dealt with by customs police stations and the policing led by them. The causes of this banditry action are very different from the causes of war. Thus, the medicine that heals the pathology of war is not the same medicine that serves to cure gang delinquency, which is organized crime.

This book, therefore, deals with those types of war divided into the three levels cited above, namely international war, civil war, and guerrilla warfare of political or religious background.

We will have to accept that war has been abolished when there are none of those three types of conflicts in the world. Commercial warfare, war of criminal factions, and war of nerves are all war in the connotative sense, not war itself. And it is of this one that we have to be rid now, because the rest will have their time.

Postwar. Can we already think of the postwar era in general?

We agreed to call "postwar" the post-1945 historical period, when World War II ended and the UN was created. Unfortunately, several wars have broken out since then, but we have no way of estimating how many more would have happened if the UN had not been acting at this stage.

If postwar refers to what came after World War II, what should we call the period that comes after the local wars cease across the globe? One possibility is "postwars". This now no longer seems like a dream.

Wars used to present recurrence. Thus, World War II was a recurrence of World War I – In its turn, Nazism, as a political doctrine, was a recurrence of the Inquisition. As it is well known, the outcome of World War I left much pending, the most notorious issue being the plan of compensation for the defeated countries. This problem and the tortuous path Germany took in setting up its reckless Weimar Republic led to the fermentation of World War II, which was driven two decades later by an injunction of the resentful militarism.

As a result of the Versailles Conference, the League of Nations was created on June 28, 1919. It was aimed at securing peace and reorganizing international relations. When beginning World War II, officially dated September 1, 1939, the diplomacy of the influential countries understood that the League of Nations had been built on the wrong bases.

It would have been a case of abandoning definitively the expectation that a society of nations could resume the work of securing peace. The mood was really like that, but an appeal by Albert Einstein for the establishment of a world government, with the United States and the then Soviet Union as its mainstay, caused the UN to be inaugurated three months later. The Security Council, a kind of permanent senate, has 15 members, who are representations of 15 countries, but only five of them are fixed. They are: United States, Russia (formerly Soviet Union), United Kingdom (England), France and China (represented by Taiwan, island of Formosa, until 1972, when it was replaced by mainland China). In September, the General Assembly meets, with representation from all member countries, which are currently 193.

First

The Great War, to come in 1914, also called World War, was predicted by many scholars in the late nineteenth century.

The Three Causes of War

In the second half of the century very significant wars unfolded on almost all the continents, and it was these various conflicts that preformed the outbreak of clash involving the Old World and the New World. It is worth mentioning the Crimean War, of France, Great Britain, Ottoman Empire (Turkey) and Sardinia against Russia, between 1853 and 1856; the Second Opium War of Great Britain, France, and the United States against China from 1956 to 1960 (the First Opium War took place from 1939 to 1942, but only Britain was fighting China, and the alliance formed in 1956 prevailed in the twentieth century); the Second Italian War of Independence. of France and Sardinia against Austria in 1859 (the First Italian War of Independence took place between 1848 and 1849); the American Civil War (the Secession Conflict), between the northern and southern United States, from 1861 to 1865; the Paraguay War (Triple Alliance War) of Brazil, Argentina and Uruguay against Paraguay, from 1864 to 1870; the Tokoshawa Shogunate Boshin War, to restore the Meiji Dynasty in Japan. From 1868 to 1869; the Franco-Prussian War, of Bavaria, Wurtemberg, Baden and the Confederation of Northern Germany against France of Napoleon III, from 1870 to 1871; the Pacific War, of Bolivia and Peru against Chile, from 1879 to 1881; the First Boer War, of Great Britain against South Africans in South Africa, from 1880 to 1881 (the Second Boer War would take place from 1899 to 1902); the First Sino-Japanese War, of Japan against China, from 1894 to 1895 (the Second Sino-Japanese War would take place from 1904 to 1905); the Spanish-American War, between the United States and Spain in dispute over the territories of Cuba and the Philippines, in 1898; and, finally, the Boxer War, of Great Britain, Russia, Japan, France, the United States, Germany, Italy, and the Austro-Hungarian Empire against China from 1900 to 1901.

With the Austro-Hungarian Empire exporting inflation to the neighborhood, the First Balkan War soon happened, while involving Serbia, Bulgaria, Montenegro and Greece against the Ottoman Empire, from 1912 to 1913. The stage for the onset of the World War began to be assembled there.

Fuse. What led the Austro-Hungarian Empire to invade Serbia?

From July 28, 1914, to November 11, 1918, the Great War developed, which after 1939 happened to be called World War I.

On June 28, 1914 members of the Austrian royal family were visiting the city of Sarajevo. A Serbian activist opposed to the interference of the Austro-Hungarian Empire in the Balkans, Gavrilo Princip, shot and killed Archduke Franz Ferdinand. In response, the Austro-Hungarian Empire gave an ultimatum to the Kingdom of Serbia, demanding greater subservience from it. The Russian Empire, twinned to Serbia by ethnic ties, since both consider themselves Slavs, profiled alongside it.

On July 28, the news was that the Austro-Hungarian Empire was beginning an invasion of Serbia, and on the same day Germany invaded Belgium, which had declared neutrality. Because of the invasion of Belgium, Britain declared war on Germany. France soon mobilized to prevent the advance of German troops over French territory. France and Britain attacked by the so-called *Western Front*, while the Russian Empire faced the Austro-Hungarian Empire from the *Eastern Front*.

There was a pact called the *Triple Alliance* between the Austro-Hungarian Empire, the German Empire, and the Kingdom of Italy, nations known as the *Central Powers*. This led to the interpretation that World War I began with a conflict between the *Triple Alliance* and the so-called *Triple Entente*, formed between the Russian Empire, France, and Great Britain. Italy, however, has moved away from the *Triple Alliance* since the outbreak of the war, on the understanding that, with the Austro-Hungarian Empire being the aggressor, the pact had been disrespected.

Although Bulgarians are also considered Slavs, this kinship did not help in a possible alignment with Russia. The Kingdom of Bulgaria and the Ottoman Empire decided to join the Austro-Hungarian Empire and the German Empire in the fight against the *Triple Entente*. On its side were the Empire of Japan, the Kingdom of Italy and the United States.

Abdication. What action did the new Russian government take in March 1917?

The conflict remained unresolved until, in early 1917, weakened by several defeats against Germany, Tsar Nicholas II, of the Romanov house, was confronted with the February Revolution and abdicated. This was followed by the Provisional Government, set up on March 15 (March 2, on their calendar, which was Julian), with Prince Georg Lvov, of the Rurikovich house, lawyer and former deputy of the Constitutional Democratic Party, as chief of State. The Provisional Government withdrew from the Great War, which made the remaining combatant countries reassess their offensives. One of the great empires of the Triple Alliance had fallen, shaken.

The arrangement with Lvov in Russia lasted, however, only four months. On July 21, another lawyer, Aleksander Kerensky, of the Social Revolutionary Party, took office. His rule lasted until November 7 (October 25 in the old calendar), when he was overthrown and replaced by the Russian Revolutionary Workers and Soldiers Committee, headed by Vladimir Lenin, who in March 1918 signed a peace agreement with the Central Powers, which Russia fought against until the beginning of the previous year. Aleksander Kerensky, exiled, died in New York in the year 1970.

Some analysts understand that, if there had not been the Russian Revolution, the Great War could have been extended for many more years. Within the so-called "war effort" actually the business of war was installed. Young men were sent to the battlefield in the same way as fighting roosters were thrown into the cockfight before the eyes of an audience of wicked elderly. Committed to preserving the lives of children, women and the elderly persons, the machinery industry was focused on producing war equipment, with guaranteed demand. The end of the war represented a redirection of the economy, leading to a period of high unemployment and even epidemics, as happened with the 1918 Spanish flu. Because these things and other motives, one already knew that, concerning war, the best possible attitude is never to start it.

Armistice. How did the end of the German monarchy occur?

What happened after the Russian Revolution was that the alliance between Britain, France, and the United States, plus the membership of Italy, Japan, Greece, Portugal, Romania, Portugal, Serbia, China, and others, including Brazil, which did not enter on the battlefield, but sent combat ships to the English Channel, intensified its attacks on Germany, the country that proved to be the leader of the Triple Alliance, although the conflict was sparked by the Austro-Hungarian Empire.

On November 4, 1918, the Austro-Hungarian Empire submitted an armistice proposal. In Germany, as early as August and September, Commanders Ludendorff and Hindenburg had been recommending surrender, assessing that the empire would inevitably be defeated. In early November, as in St. Petersburg, a workers' revolution took place in Berlin, overthrowing the monarchy and causing the Kaiser (emperor) William II to flee and go into exile in the Netherlands. On the 11th, the new German administration accepted to sign armistice, which resulted in the end of World War.

Between 1917 and 1919, the Russian Empire became the Soviet Union, the German Empire became the Weimar Republic, the Austro-Hungarian Empire, which once went from the eastern Swiss border to the Russian border. to the west, ceased to exist, separating into several countries, including Austria, Hungary, Albania and present-day Slovenia and the Czech Republic, and the Ottoman Empire, which stretched from the western border of Morocco to the eastern border of the southern Russia, encompassing northern Africa and the Middle East, including the present areas of Israel, Egypt, Gaza, Lebanon, Syria, Iraq and Jordan, all was dissolved., leaving Turkey's current territory.

On January 18, 1919, the Paris Peace Conference on war reparations began. This was the anniversary of the German Empire, officially proclaimed on January 18, 1871. The resulting document was drafted by the four big winners: Britain, France, Italy, and the United States. Finished, it was presented to the Germans as a proposed settlement on May 7 of the same year as the *Versailles Treaty*.

Nazism

The Constitution of the Weimar Republic contained a serious shortcoming, which is also found in the constitutions of other countries around the world: It did not undermine the political rights of the individual who was convicted of attempted coup. Hitler was not only arrested for the Brewery Putsch, the attempted coup d'état from Munich in 1923, but was not even a German man.

He was sentenced to five years in prison, but paid a little over one year and was released. During his time in prison, and also soon after it, he dictated his two books to his secretary Rudolf Hess and his friend Emil Maurice: "My Fight" (*Mein Kampf*) and "My Life" (*Mein Leben*).

Preaching. How did Hitler link the Jews to the idea of "race"?

In "My Fight" he expounded the Nazi doctrine, which basically spelled out the purpose of elevating Germany to be the center of the world's political power, and there elected the enemy who had been disrupting this trajectory, which was the Jewish people, through its business men, which sucked the country with exorbitant bank interest rates. To inflate the masses against the Jews in racial disagreement, he associated them with blacks, stating that the Jewish people should be persecuted because the Jewish traders were responsible for bringing the blacks to the Rhine Valley, in order to weaken their blood. German.

Blacks and Semites would therefore be inferior peoples, and should be treated as such. In the book he also stated that rarely someone emerges with the necessary leader stature to carry out such an enterprise, implying that this leader should be recognized in the figure of himself, Adolf Hitler. To clear the ground, he complained of the powerful ones of the moment, who disdained those who had no formal education, such as him, graduated only in elementary school.

Shortly after 1919, stage of approaching to the German Workers' Party (*Deutsch Arbeiter Partei*), Hitler was enchanted by the lectures of engineer Gottfried Feder, a future minister of economics in his government. Feder brought to Germany the core of the economic doctrine of proto-fascism, of rejection of international speculative capital, which compressed and reduced the forces of productive capital. Hitler's addition to that conception was the one of seeing Jewish bankers on the control of this large, invisible and oppressive factory of extortion. So the conspiracy theory that would drive the Germans crazy was formulated.

Hindenburg. How did Hindenburg try to prevent Hitler's rise?

A former arrested for attempting a coup, in 1932 Hitler launched his candidacy for the federal presidency, greatly upsetting President Hindenburg, who was ending his seven-year term. Hitler, already famous for the 1923 Putsch and for his vengeful and chauvinistic speech, had a good chance of winning the election. To prevent this, President Hindenburg agreed to run for reelection, conversely to his earlier wishes.

Marshal, hero of World War I, despite German defeat, Paul von Hindenburg was a direct descendant of Luther, and had definitively neutralized the economic Weimar Effect by settling in Berlin upon his inauguration in 1925. Germany gained industrial impulse during that first term, with the emergence and growth of automobile industry and other factories, which led to a consequent increase in volume of employment. Hitler, if elected, could keep that pace and pull glory to himself. But, ultimately, he lost the election to Hindenburg, who was reelected.

Deputy. How did Hitler circumvent defeat against Hindenburg?

Hitler's political ambition had no limits, as we all know. Seeing the dream of being elected president ruined, he decided to run for Parliament, which could be, in the impossibility of occupying the first position of the country, the second leader in the hierarchy, the chancellor of the Republic, which is what in Germany they call the office of prime minister.

In the first parliamentary election in 1932, his party, then called the National Socialist Party of German Workers, won 37% of the seats. All other competing parties were far below that, so the premier position would be up to him. Hindenburg did not agree and found a way to cancel the competition and call another, weeks later, making it clear to the Germans that the result, by hitting Hitler as main postulant to the position of chief of government, was not approved. However, in this second election, without the president to have enough time to inform the voter, Hitler's party got 32% of the seats. Hindenburg then proceeded to work out an agreement between the Communist Party and the Catholic Party, the two major forces opposing the Nazis. Twenty-eight parties were elected (political Weimar Effect), and with 68% of the seats out of Nazi hands it would be very easy to form an alliance if these other deputies had a crystal ball to predict the misfortune Hitler was bringing, or if they had the perception clear from Hindenburg that Hitler was a politician of bad character.

Premier. Who advised Hindenburg to inaugurate Hitler?

Hindenburg wore a lot trying to join disparate forces against Hitler. After many unsuccessful attempts, he was advised by former Center Party premier Franz von Papen to take over Hitler. After all, the Chancellors of the Republic lasted very little time in the post, and soon Germany would be free of the Austrian. The president gave up, and in 1933 Hitler began his rule.

One of the first measures of the new government was to decree dismissal from the public service of any official identified as Jewish. Albert Einstein, who after much insistence from Max Plank, had accepted a few years earlier to engage in the University of Berlin, was one of the Jews hit by that measure.

On August 2 of the following year, 1934, Hindenburg passed away.

Prior to that, in March, the chief of government withdrew German citizenship from all Jews in the country. And on June 30, in response, according to the Nazis themselves, to a Jew's murder in Paris, came the Night of the Long Daggers, with brutal attacks on Jewish-owned shops, resulting in hundreds of deaths. All these events, and perhaps others of which we are not yet aware, led to the death of the old marshal, which opened the way for dictatorship for Hitler.

Had he had any nobleness of character, even much ambitious,

Hitler would have presented his name to Parliament to run for the presidential seat, providing a replacement for the post of prime minister in the case he was elected to the top post. What he did, however, was very consistent with his temperament. He called for the "self-nomination" plebiscite, in which the Germans would answer Yes or No to his claim to be self-nominated as federal president, while maintaining his position as chief of government. It would be a referendum of extinction of parliamentarism.

President. How much support did Hitler have to become chief of State?

With a year of rule, at that time the Germans imagined that Hitler would be the right man to continue German economic growth. His victory in the referendum was 88%.

Sworn in as top leader, he began to pursue his claims for Germany's expansion.

The first act of counteracting the Treaty of Versailles and the League of Nations was the Saarland plebiscite, in January 1935. The Saarland is an administrative unit created by the Treaty of Versailles on the German border with Luxembourg and France , with just over 2,500 km², and that, since 1919, was being governed by the League of Nations. Today it could be a UN territory, perhaps its government headquarters. But Hitler's consultation there resulted in 90% support for incorporation into Germany. It was the first defeat of the League of Nations and undoubtedly the foreshadowing of its dissolution.

From then on Hitler refused to see any world authority above his own. In March, he decreed the formation of the Air Force and the restoration of the compulsory military service. In the following days, he turned a blind eye to the League of Nations act that condemned those rearmament decisions, contrary to the decisions of the Treaty of Versailles. The entity continued to issue condemnation notes to Nazi acts, but its voice was becoming ever smaller. On August 31, the United States government proclaimed its Neutrality Act, leaving Hitler at ease to act in Europe. Although many US Jews were clamoring for an anti-Nazi stance on the part of the country, the industry had been gaining a lot from Germany's economic recovery, providing machinery and equipment and installing powerful multinationals there, which had been helping a lot to overcome the Great Crash of 1929.

Pacts. How did the cooperation between Hitler and Mussolini begin?

In July 1936, days after the outbreak of the Spanish Civil War, Hitler and Mussolini sent military equipment to Francisco Franco's rebels. Such action led to the agreement that was signed in Berlin by the Italian Chancellery in October and proclaimed in Rome by Mussolini, in the so-called *Rome-Berlin Pact*, in November. That same month, Italy and Germany recognized Francisco Franco's coup government. Still in November Germany and Japan signed the *Antikomintern Pact*, which received Italy's accession the following year.

In March 1938, the Germans entered Vienna and soon declared the *Anschluss* (the annexation). On 29 September the *Munich Conference* was held between Hitler, Chamberlain (England), Mussolini (Italy) and Daladier (France). The following day the *Munich Agreements* were signed, granting for Germany the right to annex the Sudeten region, whose majority was German in Czechoslovakia, which had been insisting on the passage of the territory to German jurisdiction. In October the Germans took over the region.

Earlier the following year Hitler's ally Francisco Franco took Barcelona and showed his military superiority in the *Spanish Civil War*, having his government recognized by France and England. The seizure of Madrid would come on April 1st. In March of that year, 1939, the Germans took Czechoslovakia, which months earlier had incorporated Hungary. In the same month Hitler began to claim the German possession of Dantzig (Gdansk), which was in Polish hands.

While celebrating among his helpers and friends his great advances in those days, Hitler at his country house showed a grave concern. He said, "If Churchill wins the British election, we'll be in trouble."

It can be said that even before the official date of the beginning of World War II, on September 1, the world was conflagrated. Beyond the Spanish Civil War, a very bloody battle between Arabs and Jews was taking place in the British protectorate of the territory that would become the State of Israel, subtracted from Turkey in 1917, after its defeat in World War I. Italy, which had already taken Abyssinia in Africa, was now invading and incorporating Albania, in April. In the East, Japan had been warring with China for several months, and, in May, it also fought against Russia, then part of the Soviet Union, on the border with Mongolia. Hitler, counting on a substantial weakening of the Russians on the eastern side, instructed his chancellery to sign the German-Soviet non-aggression agreement, which took place in the *Molotov-Ribbentrop Pact*, on August 23. The following day, trusting in that initiative, President Franklin Delano Roosevelt and Pope Pius XII made Hitler an appeal for world peace.

Neither Roosevelt nor Pius XII said explicitly in their message, but Hitler's request not to invade Poland was implicit. The invasion, however, was nonnegotiable to the head of the German government.

German troops invaded Poland on September 1, bombed Warsaw, Lodz, and Krakow, and the next day seized Dantzig.

Chapter 2 - Recurrence

That World War II was a recurrence of World War I is not much doubt. But it is also possible to understand that World War I was a recurrence of the Franco-Prussian War, of 1871. With the defeat inflicted on Napoleon III, who wanted to annex Luxembourg, by Bismark, who won to Germany the French territory of Alsace-Lorraine, at the end of the conflict, the Germans may have developed the conviction that future battles between Germany and France would give them the victory. And if they lost, as in World War I, a rematch would settle the matter. Obviously, all this is speculation, but social psychology is a clear science.

At the Versailles Conference, young economist John Maynard Keynes worked on the British team. After the treaty was drafted, he decided to withdraw and return to London, refusing to sign the document, claiming that sanctions on losers were very foolish and would lead to a new conflict at the earliest opportunity. Bertrand Russell, his friend and senior colleague at Cambridge University, wrote in some books that World War II was being prepared.

The digressions and information above serve to relativize the centrality of the Hitler's unhealthy profile. In 1919 Keynes could not imagine that a cable of Austrian origin, probably mutilated from war (many say Hitler was shot in the genitals during a battle), would emerge insufflating and rearming Germany for a new conflict. But he saw that some strong leadership could, with considerable chance, enlist humiliated forces for great revenge. At that time he was preparing his doctoral thesis, to be presented in 1921, entitled "Treatise on Probability."

Hyperinflation. Which banker gave clout to Hitler's rise?

What could not be predicted was Germany's rapid economic growth, even subject to the drastic restrictions of the Versailles Treaty. This growth, much more than a reaction to the victors of World War I, was the result of a positive response to the Weimar Republic disaster, which, although officially dissolved only in 1933, with Hitler coming to power, 15 years after its creation, in November 1918, its ill-fated period occurred between 1919 and 1923, as it was plunged into hyperinflation of unprecedented dimensions in world history.

Even being the beginning of monetary stabilization considered the launching of the currency Rentenmark, by Reischbank President Hjalmar Schacht, in November 1923, and one calls that event "Rentenmark miracle", under the presidency of Friedrich Ebert, who ruled the country from 1919 to 1925, it was only with Hindenburg's arrival as president that the economy gained pulse. Together with Franz von Papen, Hjalmar Schacht endorsed Hitler's rise in 1932, and was later awarded with the post of Minister of Economy, from 1934 to 1937.

After spending a few years under hyperinflation, the productive impulse that the country acquired by getting rid of it compares with the force of a gigantic dike that has accumulated water constantly throughout that period and only then can make use of it. It is true that hyperinflation impoverishes everyone, rich, medium and poor, but the moment of monetary stabilization brings the entrepreneurial animal spirit to unimaginable heights. All the desire to invest and produce, dammed by the inflationary years, is exposed without fear and without reservations. A terrible disease, which is hyperinflation, is followed by a true sense of miracle.

Poland. What happened in England shortly after Hitler invaded Poland?

It was in this climate that Hitler felt comfortable for invading Poland on September 1 and, on day 2, taking Dantzig.

On September 3, however, Winston Churchill became part of the British government. On the same day, India, New Zealand, and Australia declared war on Germany. The United States reaffirmed their neutrality, followed by Japan the next day. It is important to remember that while Japan's chancellery and imperial cabinet were allied with the United States, as in World War I, the General Staff and the chancellery secretly was backing plans in contrary sense.

On the 9th, Canada, another Commonwealth member, also declared war on Germany. Meanwhile the Germans consolidated their positions in Poland, Japan established an armistice with the Soviet Union, which, on the 17th, invaded also Poland from the west side, taking advantage of the weakening to which the Nazis had already subjected it.

On November 8 Hans Frank was appointed governor-general of Poland, imposing on the country Nazi doctrine. On the 30th, it was the Soviet Union's turn to attack Finland, bombarding the capital Helsinki, prompting the League of Nations to expel it from its ranks the following month.

In January 1940, Denmark, Norway, and Sweden declared

neutrality, but Churchill appealed to those who remained neutral to join the Allies against Nazi expansion. The Pope, on the 22nd, issued a note condemning Nazi abuse in Poland.

In late February Sweden banned the transit of Allied troops on its territory, which was not followed by Norway and Denmark and already on March 1 Hitler ordered the invasion of these two nations.

On May 10 the Germans invaded Belgium, the Netherlands and Luxembourg. On the same date, Neville Chamberlain fell, in London, after ordering the invasion of Iceland, and Churchill was appointed prime minister. On the 13th he made the historic speech to Parliament, saying that he could offer only "blood, sweat and tears". The Auschwitz concentration camp went into operation next week, on the 20th.

On June 3, German aviation bombed Paris, and on June 5 the French government, formed by Reynaud, Petain, Daladier and Mandel, appointed Charles De Gaulle as Undersecretary of State for Defense. Faced with Nazi advances in France and attacks on southern England, on the 7th British aviation bombed Berlin. On the 10th, Italy declared war on the United Kingdom and France, while invading southern France and being expelled by the Allies. On the 12th, however, it bombarded Lyon. On the 14th the Nazis seized Paris and the French government settled in Bordeaux.

On the 12th, Reynaud resigned from the government and Marshal Philippe Petain formed a new cabinet. On the 17th he announced that he requested an armistice from the German government. At this surrender, the British government recognized General Charles De Gaulle as head of the Free French Forces.

In Japan, a new government was installed on the 22nd, with General Tojo Hideki as minister of war and Matsuoka Yosuke as minister of foreign affairs. Yosuke graduated as a lawyer in the United States, but later developed a great aversion to the country.

Vichy. How did francophone countries see the Vichy government?

On July 1, 1940, the French government settled in the city of Vichy, sealing that day the beginning of the downward curve of the Nazi life cycle, as we will see shortly. On the 10th, the Vichy Assembly invested Pétain with full power over France, which inaugurated Collaborationist France. The next day, the marshal was appointed chief of State, in fact, of a tutored state.

Still in July, on the 24th, the Germans tried to invade England using airplanes and ships, but were repelled. That month, several French-speaking countries allied with De Gaulle, refusing to recognize Vichy's government. Meanwhile, Romania has allied with the Germans.

On August 2nd the Vichy Government judged De Gaulle a rebel general and, by default, sentenced him to death. Also earlier that month, Estonia, Latvia and Lithuania, which had been under attack by the Russians, became Soviet republics.

On the 28th the night bombing against British cities were begun, reaching London, Liverpool, Manchester and several others. London's response was to bomb Berlin again.

In September, bombings continued on London, including attacks on the Parliament building.

British. How did Alan Turing crack the Nazi missile code?

A group of scientists, including the 26-year-old young mathematician Alan Turing, has begun studies from the Polish resistance intelligence service to crack Nazi codes for missile fire. Alan Turing and Gordon Welchman designed a powerful calculator, which they named "The Bomb", intended to help unravel the operation of the machine "Enigma", used by the Nazis. Decisions about the bombing were made by Enigma, and even its operating officers could not predict what it would determine. In three months of working with The Bomb, Turing, a doctor of cryptology, achieved to solve the problem. Many thousands of lives were saved, because from there the Nazi attacks were no longer a secret. After the war, Turing, a homosexual, agreed to undergo hormone treatment to be presented as a hero, without violating British that punished homosexual acts with imprisonment. It was long believed that the then rudimentary treatment led to his death when he was 41year-old. Subsequently, maybe by convenience of State, a consensus was formed that he died by suicide, poisoning himself.

Still in September 1940, on the 23rd, Japan invaded Indochina (Vietnam, Laos and Cambodia), which belonged to France. On the 25th, the United States began to restrict oil exports to the Japanese, and on the 27th, Japan signed with Italy and Germany the Tripartite Pact, known as the *Rome-Berlin-Tokyo Axis*.

On October 28th Italy invaded Greece and the next day British troops landed on the island of Crete.

On November 5th Roosevelt was reelected in the United States and his speech in those days was of assistance to all who fought against the Axis, that is, against Nazi-fascism.

In 1941, on January 7th, the Japanese army commander proposed in a memorandum a surprise attack on Pearl Harbor, Hawaii, which is part of the United States. Nazi air strikes on London continued. The British responded by bombing several German cities. At the end of February, they took Somalia in East Africa, which was being colonized by Italy.

In the months that followed, great battles took place in North Africa and the Balkans. Although the British regained Eritrea, the Germans, who already dominated Greece, while succeeding Italy, seized Yugoslavia, driving away King Peter II, who was an ally of the British. Bulgaria and Romania already were aligned with the Axis.

In the Arabian Peninsula the Kingdom of Iraq had declared support for the Axis, but the British carried out several attacks on the country and caused the monarch to flee to Germany, with the Iraqis signing an armistice with the United Kingdom.

Russia. In the Siege of Leningrad, how many starved to death each day?

Hitler saw in the British resistance a road accident that would hinder, but not prevent, the Nazi expansion plan. Thus, on June 25th, the Continuing War began, with Germans and Finns fighting against the Soviet Union. The next day Mussolini sent divisions in support of the Nazis in this offensive, and on the 30th Vichy France broke off relations with the Soviets.

Throughout July the Germans seized Latvia, Belarus and Bessarabia and on the 24th bombed Moscow. In attack on Smolensk they arrested Yákov Dzhugashvili, son of Stalin.

In the offensives against Leningrad (St. Petersburg), the former capital of Russia, and Kiev, the capital of Ukraine, as well as against other major cities, the Germans' strategy was to prevent the arrival of food, thus starving many thousands of Soviets. .

On July 27th, Japanese troops entered Saigon, Indochina (Vietnam), and on the 29th signed an agreement with Collaborationist France to split the defense of the then colony.

On August 25th British and Soviet troops entered Tehran, expelling the Shah (emperor), who favored the Axis, and swearing in his son, Mohammad Reza Pahlevi, as the new Shah of Persia (Iran).

On October 4th, the United States stopped exporting oil to Japan, a detail that would be used by the Tojo government, installed on the 16th of the same month, as a justification for the growing hostilities against Franklin Roosevelt.

In early October the Soviets removed women and children from

Moscow, while troops defeated successive Nazi attacks. At the end of the month winter came to the city with very low temperatures, which helped the Russians, accustomed to that situation.

In November, under the Siege of Leningrad, the number of people starving to death each day was estimated at 400.

On December 5th, aided by "general" winter, as in the previous century in relation to Napoleon Bonaparte, the Russians definitively expelled the Germans from the outskirts of Moscow. The game began to turn in favor of the Soviets.

Hawaii. What day of 1940 did the Pearl Harbor attack occur?

Two days later, December 7th, after the German defeat in Moscow, Rommel also began the withdrawal of Nazi troops from North Africa. The Japanese reacted to these setbacks in a harsh and seemingly desperate manner, but also, most likely, to take the place of the Germans in leading the Axis. They attacked the US military base in Peal Harbor, Hawaii, and then declared war on the United States, Great Britain, Canada, and Australia. Still on the 7th, occupied the international zone of Shanghai.

On the 8th, they attacked Hong Kong and invaded the Philippines and Malaysia. The following day, December 9th, China declared war on Germany and Italy, and on the 13th the Japanese occupied Guam Island, which was another US base in the Pacific Ocean.

On December 22nd Churchill met with Roosevelt in Washington to establish a joint General Staff for the Axis War. The same day the United States bombed Davao in the Philippines. From that day on, the United States became participants in the war, not only with material and financial support, but with troops.

Midway. What feat did the United States accomplish at the *Battle of Midway*?

In 1942, on January 3rd, the Allied Forces appointed General Chiang Kai-Shek as their commander in Chinese territory. On February 11th, at a meeting in Seville, Salazar, Portugal's premier, and Franco, dictator of Spain, declared their countries neutral in the world conflict. On May 12th, David Ben-Gurion issues a statement in favor of the creation of a state for Jews around Jerusalem. Later that month, the Japanese conquered Burma (Myanmar) and secured various positions in the Philippines, China and Southeast Asia. The Germans regained strength and reconquered positions in Ukraine, while Rommel launched an offensive to secure control of Libya.

On June 1, the Treblinka extermination camp began operations, and on the 7th, the United States sank Japan's carrier fleet at the *Battle of Midway*, beginning the breakdown of Japanese power in the Pacific Ocean. On the 25th General Eisenhower arrived in England to command the US troops that were based there.

With the Germans again attacking areas of the Soviet Union, on July 17th the Battle of Stalingrad (Volgograd) began, resulting in about two million deaths on both sides of the conflict.

That year of 1942 the struggle for independence against Britain intensified in India. On August 9th riots in various parts of the then colony led to the arrest of leading independentist leaders, including Gandhi and Nehru. Demonstrations continued the following day, resulting in bloody riots.

Weeks after Mexico's entry into the war, on August 22nd, because of a Nazi attack on a Brazilian-flagged merchant ship, Brazil declared war on Germany and Italy.

Days after a meeting of Laval and Hitler, before the fiasco of the French government in Vichy, on November 10th France was occupied by German and Italian troops. On the 18th, Marshal Pétain had to officially hand over power to Laval. By then, Vichy had morally destroyed Nazism.

International. Why did Stalin dissolve the III International?

In 1943, the siege of Stalingrad was broken by the Russians, on January 11th, and on the 16th the English resumed their attacks on Berlin, reinforced by the announcement that Iraq, once dominated by the Germans, was declaring war on the Axis. The siege of Leningrad (St. Petersburg) was broken on the 18th, by Soviet forces. Under heavy Allied Forces attacks, on the 21st the Germans fled Tripoli, the capital of Libya.

Field Marshal Friedrich Paulus, commander of the Nazi forces at the Battle of Stalingrad, asked Hitler for permission to surrender, but was denied him the demand. Days later, on January 31, he was arrested by the Russians, which ended the German offensive in that city.

On February 19th Goebbels announced in Berlin the "total war". But on the 20th, as a sign of the weakening of the Axis forces and their power of persuasion, Fiat workers, in Italy, began the first political strike against the fascist regime. In the same month, a small Norwegian command, in the Operation Gunnerside, attacked and disabled the German-owned heavy water production plant at Norsk Hydro, thereby preventing a possible manufacture of Nazi atomic bombs.

On March 13th German officials installed a bomb on a plane on which Hitler would travel. It was another sign that Nazism was in decline. The artifact, however, did not explode due to some defect. That same day the transfer of Jews from the Krakow ghetto to extermination camps was begun. The more Nazism realized its vulnerability, the more cruel was the response to those who were subjected to them.

In those days the attacks of the United States forces on Naples, Palermo and other Italian cities intensified. On April 18th, US fighters attacked the plane on which Japanese commander Isoroku Yamamoto was traveling, killing him with the crash of the aircraft.

On May 15th, in gesture of goodwill, Stalin dissolved the Communist International (III International, or III International Workers' Association), which was an entity that prevented agreements between the Soviets and the Western Allied Forces, since its purpose was to expand the proletarian revolution around the world, with the overthrow of constituted governments.

Mussolini. How was Mussolini fired from the premier post?

In June, the 3rd, 1943, there was a setback for the Allies in South America, with Colonel Juan Domingos Perón, sympathetic to Nazi fascism, seizing power in Argentina through a coup d'état.

On July 13th, Tito's guerrillas, while fighting against the Nazis in the Balkans, proclaimed the Democratic Republic of Croatia. The next day, de Gaulle declared that Algiers, North Africa, became the provisional capital of France.

With some Italian cities already taken over by the Allies and others under heavy bombardment, King Victor Emmanuel III summoned Mussolini to a meeting on July 25th, but as soon as the Duce entered the limousine, he was arrested. He was removed from the post of prime minister and in his place the monarch appointed Pietro Badoglio. The next day riots in the city of Milan resulted in the deaths of over 200 Mussolini supporters. On the 28th the Fascist Party was officially extinguished. The German government lost this important ally to the west, but on the 30th it sent eight divisions to confront the "Campaign of Italy" troops, which fought the Nazi-fascists in the territory.

On August 17th, the Allies completely dominated Sicily, continuing to bombard several other Italian cities. It was not until the 19th that the country's government decided to sit at the table to negotiate the armistice with the allies. This, however, did not mean the end of Allied attacks on cities that still remained under the Axis rule.

On September 8th the armistice came into force, but on the 9th the Germans advanced on Rome, causing the royal family and the prime minister to flee to Brindisi. Even so, Princess Mafalda and her husband Felipe de Hesse-Kassel were arrested and sent to a concentration camp. It became clear that Mussolini, like Petain in Vichy, ruled as a German employee. But that same day, Persia (Iran), in the hands of Shah Mohammed Reza Pahlevi, declared war on Germany, reinforcing the Allied Forces side.

Eisenhower. What day of 1943 did Eisenhower become supreme commander?

On the 12th a Nazi command rescued Mussolini from the prison in Gran Sasso. The next day Chiang Kai-Shek, a trusted Allied Forces general, was elected president of China. To his misfortune, he did not exercise government in Beijing, but in Nanjing, which no longer had secular national capital status.

On the 23rd, with Nazi help Mussolini proclaimed his Italian Social Republic in Saló, which became known as the Republic of Saló. For this it had to give to the Germans the regions of Trieste, Fiume, Istria and Alto Adige.

In Naples, on September 28th, the popular uprising against the Nazi occupation began, in what became known as the Four Days of Naples.

On October 13th, the Italian government declared war on Germany, but the Nazis continued to rule Rome and mainly arrest the city's Jews. On the 24th they bombed Naples, which had been taken over by the Allied Forces earlier this month, after the popular uprising. On the 30th, Badoglio signed the return of the democratic freedoms and political parties in Italy.

On November 27th, after having a submarine attacked by Nazis, Colombia declared war on Germany. The next day the first conference between Stalin, Franklin Roosevelt and Churchill took place in Tehran.

On December 4th, a government of the liberated area in the Balkans, Yugoslavia, was formed, with Tito as provisional president. On the 15th, the United States, the United Kingdom, and the Soviet Union recognized the Tito's presidency.

On the 17th, Captain Axel von dem Bussche attempted a suicide bombing against Hitler, but the bomb blast did not reach the Nazi leader.

On the 24th, Christmas Eve, the Allied Forces appointed

Eisenhower as supreme commander of the forces fighting Nazi-fascism throughout Europe.

Victor. Who succeeded Victor Emmanuel on the throne of Italy?

The first week of 1944 brought strong indications that World War II was nearing its end, with the pendulum favoring the Allied Forces, which, however, were aware that victory would still cost a lot of "blood, sweat and tear". .

On January 1, the British Royal Air Force used 700 aircraft to bomb Berlin, repeating the operation on day 2, the day US troops began to conquer the Japanese naval base of Rabaul. On the 3rd, the English bombed Turin, and on the 4th, the United States bombed Dupnitsa, in Bulgaria, a country whose monarch was Prince Simeon, six, since half a year earlier his father, King Boris III, died while was coming back from a meeting with Hitler, to settle details of Bulgarian support for the Nazis.

On the 5th, US forces bombed Dusseldorf and Bordeaux, as well as other important German and French cities. Over the next few days and weeks the bombing by the Allied Forces continued, because it was necessary to ensure the gradual weakening of the Nazi fascist bases.

Until this early 1944, and since July 1, 1940, with the establishment of the Vichy regime in France, the world did not know a day without a bombing on any city or military base. The war would be won by he who could add more territory, more weapons production and greater use of military intelligence. With the Declaration of Neutrality of Portugal and Spain, the Germans seemed to have dominated the whole of western Europe, after the occupation of France. If they defeated Stalin and incorporated the Soviet Union, all of continental Europe would be Nazi, and dominating Britain would only be a matter of time and patience.

It was not the case of blaming the Nazi officers' calculations. Everything for them was fine. They simply forgot to take into account the power of the notorious Russian "general winter", and completely ignored the corrosive action of the Ravenna Effect, which had already benefited them in the form of the Weimar Effect, when Schacht lent Hitler his prestige and his clout as artificer of the German monetary stabilization of 1923, but now it was coated with a more devastating new color: the Vichy regime. Weeks after Marshal Pétain's Nazi-fascist government was installed there, not in Paris, practically all French colonies and former colonies aligned with the Resistance. Not that General De Gaulle had an irresistible charisma. Quite the opposite. The stampede against Petain was due to his artificial regime in the city of Vichy.

As a result of the Verona Process on the 11th, five fascist leaders were executed: Cyan, Marinelli, Gottardi, Pairschi and Marshal Emilio de Bono. Other leaders managed to escape.

On the 17th the Battle of Montecassino began.

On the 24th, the Soviet Red Army finally broke the siege of Leningrad, driving away the Germans, in action completed on February 14th.

In Indochina, Ho Chi-Min proclaimed, on March 28th, the Provisional Government of the Republic of Vietnam.

On May 19th the Battle of Montecassino ended, with the victory of the Allied Forces.

On June 4th, the Allied Forces entered Rome, disrupting the Nazis, and the next day King Victor Emmanuel III abdicated in favor of his son, Prince Umberto of Saboya.

D-Day

On June 6th, the Allied Forces landed in Normandy during Operation Overlord. The fact became known as *D-Day*. However, the plan was discovered by the Nazis, who countered, shooting down more than 900 planes in combat on the 13th. Even in the face of this adversity, the offensive continued and proved decisive in the attack. outcome of the world conflict.

On the 20th, Soviet troops entered Finland, which had not accepted Moscow's armistice proposal.

On the 22nd, the British Royal Air Force bombarded the German-held areas of Normandy with 600 aircraft.

On the 26th, by miscalculation, British forces bombed the Republic of San Marino, located in northeastern Italy. On the same day, US planes attacked Vienna, this time with no miscalculations.

On July 1 the Bretton Woods Accords began in the United States. There, at the suggestion of John Maynard Keynes, the International Monetary Fund (IMF) was created, with initial participation of 44 countries. The World Bank was also created, and it would be headed by US-appointed technicians, while the IMF would be run by French. The World Trade Organization (WTO) was proposed by Eugenio Gudin, but Keynes thought it was too early for the launch of such an entity, which would not materialize until 1968.

On the 5th, the British bombed Dijon, while US forces attacked Montpellier and Tolon. The same day the Russians regained Minsk, the capital of Belarus. On the 15th, the United States resumed Guam base in the Pacific.

On the 20th, Colonel Claus von Stauffenberg carried out a bomb attack (Operation Valkyrie) against Hitler, but the plan failed and those involved were executed.

On August 1, the Red Army, which after defeating the Germans in St. Petersburg continued westward advances, arrived in Warsaw, Poland. Hitler, knowing about this, ordered the total destruction of the city by Nazi troops.

On the 20th the Germans arrested Marshal Petain in Vichy, leading him to Belfort, and on the 25th General Dietrich von Chollitz signed the capitulation of the German troops in Paris, handing over the city command to General Leclerc.

Here we had the most significant milestone in the Nazis' downward trajectory: The Allied reconquest of Paris on August 25th, 1944. After that, Hitler's defeat would be a matter of weeks or days.

Paris. What political lines formed the government of France with De Gaulle?

On September 1, reaffirming the importance of the reconquest of Paris, Eisenhower transferred the command of the Allied Forces to General Montgomery and changed headquarters to France. On the same day another Allied bombing, the second, was dumped on Tokyo. The base of Iwo Jima was also attacked.

Realizing that it had been alone, on the 2nd Finland broke off diplomatic relations with Germany. On the 3rd, the English occupied Brussels, and De Gaulle's forces, with the help of the United States, resumed Lyon.

On the 9th, a new French government was formed, based in Paris and led by De Gaulle, bringing together liberals and communists.

On the 10th US soldiers entered German territory, but judged premature to advance to Berlin. On the 19th, Finland and the Soviet Union signed a peace treaty, and the next day the Allied troops liberated the Republic of San Marino, which had been occupied by exaggerated precaution.

Facing the advance of the Allied Forces on the western side and the Red Army on the eastern side, the Nazis played their last cards. On September 25th Hitler summoned all 14 to 60-year-old men to war.

On the 29th Tito signed with Stalin an agreement releasing Yugoslav territory for any Red Army operations against the Germans.

On October 1 the German withdrawal from Athens began and the division under siege in Calais, France, surrendered to the Allied Forces. On the 9th, the Nazis began their withdrawal from Hungary.

On the 14th Erwin Rommel committed suicide, when he was alerted that he was about to be tried as one of the participants in the planning of the July attack on Hitler.

On October 31 the Royal British Air Force continued the bombing begun the day before over the city of Cologne. On the same day the Germans finally abandoned their positions in Greece.

On November 7th, the Nazis began their withdrawal from the entire Italian Peninsula.

For the remainder of the year, daily attacks continued to occur. The Soviets were advancing as they resumed positions in the Balkans and assisted their ally Tito of Yugoslavia. The United States was trying to free the Philippines and regain Pacific positions against the Japanese forces, but they were attacked by kamikazes, the suicide pilots who died in the name of the emperor. As the Axis dominated most of Europe and most of the Pacific, the work of territorial recovery would have to be slow. Much of the effort went into attacks on vehicle factories, including warplanes, and on weapons and fuel. On the last day of 1944 British aviation succeeded in completely destroying Gestapo headquarters in its Oslo section, and the new Hungarian government declared war on Germany.

Yalta. What world leaders joined in the Yalta Conference?

On January 1, 1945, with the arrival of the Red Army in East Prussia, Nazi troops retreated. On the same day US forces carried out another bombing of Tokyo.

By the planning of the D-Day invasion, the war should not have lasted until 1945, but the Germans' unexpected retaliation in Normandy showed that they still had garrisons and equipment for many months of battle. The conflict would have to continue until the annihilation of the Nazi forces, because Hitler's fanaticism and his rule over the Germans were well known.

On January 7th, 900 British airplanes bombed Munich at night, and on the 8th, over 1,000 Allied Forces aircraft bombed Frankfurt.

Also from Warsaw the Germans began to drift away with the arrival of the Soviets, on the 14th, leaving the city definitively on the 16th.

On the 18th the Soviets entered Silesia and on the same day the provisional government of Poland settled in the capital, Warsaw, coming from Lublin.

On the 27th the Red Army seized the Auschwitz concentration camp and released the prisoners, which were about 7,000. The next day the Soviets entered Pomerania.

On February 3rd, the Allied Forces declared Belgium's total release from German rule. On the same day US forces seized Manila, the capital of the Philippines, which was still under Japanese rule.

The following day, February 4th, the Yalta Conference between Franklin Roosevelt, Winston Churchill and Iosif Stalin began to discuss the new political relations between the major states of the world after the end of the war, which was already drawn up.

In February several countries that remained neutral declared war on the Axis, including Saudi Arabia, which made the announcement on the 10th. Peru made the equivalent declaration on the 12th, the day the Yalta Conference also closed.

Sunset How did Hitler die on April 30, 1945?

On the 19th Himmler began negotiations with Swedish authorities with a view to a settlement ending the war, unlike Hitler.

On the 20th the Soviets took Dantzig (Gdansk).

On February 23rd the bombing of Berlin began. On the same day, US forces, after several kamikaze attacks, climbed Mount Suribachi on Iwo Jima and raised the flag of their country in symbolic gesture of victory. The kamikazes continued the attacks for a few more weeks.

In March the bombings on Berlin became daily.

On April 8th the Soviets seized Konigsberg, and on 10th US troops occupied Essen and Hannover.

On the 11th, US forces released the prisoners from Buchenwald concentration camp, and on that day the Soviets seized the city of Vienna, while Tito's army seized Sarajevo.

On the 12th, President Franklin Roosevelt passed away, being replaced by Harry Truman, which did not alter the politics of war. On the 13th, US forces seized Iena, Weimar, and Erfurt.

On April 16th the Soviets arrived in Berlin, and daily Allied Forces attacks were halted, so as not to conflict with Red Army action in the city. On the 17th the US air force began bombing Dresden. The city was completely destroyed in the following days.

On the 20th, US forces occupied Nuremberg. Meanwhile the

Soviets bombarded Berlin intensely, preparing the occupation.

On April 25th, the San Francisco Conference signed its intention to found the UN, which would be officially established months later, on the second semester.

On March 26th Marshal Pétain was arrested by the Allied Forces and on the same day Mussolini tried to flee from Italy, dressed as a German soldier, with a Nazi entourage, but the next day he was intercepted by anti-fascist guerrillas while trying to enter Switzerland.

On the 28th, Communist guerrillas shot Mussolini and his companion Clara Petacci. They were taken, along with other fascist leaders also shot, to Loreto Square, in Milan, where they were tied up and exposed upside down. The population attacked the bodies with everything in front of them, leaving their faces disfigured.

On the 29th US troops took over the Dachau concentration camp. That same day Hitler married Eva Braun and, by default, appointed Donitz as his successor.

On the 30th Hitler locked himself in his quarters with his wife Eva Braun and, after hearing gunshots, assistants opened the door and saw that both were dead. Officially, it was recognized that Hitler committed suicide.

Kamikazes. When was the last kamikaze attack on American troops?

On May 1, Magda Goebbels killed her six children by poison. After that, she was shot and killed by her husband, Joseph Goebbels, who then committed suicide. Hitler bunker runners organized breakouts of the site, in groups. Hitler had left orders for his body to be incinerated, which appears to have been fulfilled by his guards.

On day 2nd Donitz took office as Hitler's successor, but this was a purely protocol act, because on the same day Germany's capitulation to the Soviet forces took place. The Donitz government lasted 23 hours. Still on day 2nd, the Germans resisting in Italy surrendered, and the Allied Forces took about one million Nazi prisoners.

Japan, however, did not give in. On day 3rd its air force carried out another powerful attack on the Allied forces occupying it. On the 6th, recognizing the German capitulation, it ended the Tripartite Pact, which formed the Axis, but persisted in the war effort. On the 10th, US forces resumed the bombing of Tokyo as a deterrent. The response was a strong kamikaze attack on the Allied base in Okinawa the next day.

In the following days intense bombing of US forces was dumped over Tokyo, but also over Yokohama, Nagoya, Osaka, and Kobe. Meanwhile, Japanese forces continued to attack Okinawan-based US troops.

On June 1, Greece and Brazil declared war on Japan in support of the United States.

On the 21st the conquest of Okinawa by the United States was completed. One last kamikaze attack took place that day. In those weeks after the German surrender, the Chinese also regained many cities that were still under Japanese rule.

On July 5th, General MacArthur declared that the Philippines was finally released from Japanese rule. From Iwo Jima, US forces continued to bomb Tokyo.

On the 13th, Italy declared war on Japan. On that day, with the arrival of British troops in Berlin to join the Soviets, the Victory Parade was held there.

On the 16th, the United States detonated the first atomic bomb as a test in Alamogordo, New Mexico State. The next day Truman, Churchill, and Stalin met at the Potsdam Conference to discuss Germany's future.

Atomic. What happened to Japan on August 6, 1945?

On August 6th, US forces blew up the first atomic bomb on a city. In this attack on Hirohima, more than 100,000 people died. Two days later the Soviet Union invaded Manchukuo, declaring war on Japan. No sign of surrender came from the Japanese, and on the 9th US forces detonated the second atomic bomb, this time over the city of Nagasaki, killing about 36,000 people immediately and leaving more than 40,000 injured.

On the 15th, Emperor Hiroite made the decision to declare the Japanese surrender.

The act was signed September 2nd aboard the battleship Missouri. Only on that day, World War II finished, in practice and officially.

On October 24th, the United Nations Charter was signed in San Francisco. The Paris Conference, to discuss the reparations to be imposed on Germany, began on November 9th, and on the 14th the Nuremberg Court began trial proceedings against war criminals.

Method

In the 1944 book "The Road to Serfdom", Friedrich Hayek

explains in the chapter "Why the Worst Get on Top", how the Nazis rallied the masses in favor of their beliefs, making Hitler finally reach the position of chief of government. He wrote that if one tries to bring people together to do some noble cause, to help people in need, for example, it has little effect, but if the call is to foment hatred for a person or a cause, then the possibility of growth of the campaign is high.

The book presents a good analysis, but fails to use a psychological category of personal relationships, hate, to explain a mass phenomenon. The author confuses hate with method.

When a judge condemns a culprit, applying the appropriate penalties to him, he does not make the decision based on hatred, but in compliance with current law. Hate may be present in the sentence, but here we have a case of judge who mixes profession with intimate life. And what is the difference between the action of the judge who punishes the guilty and that of the political militant who, participating in a punisher doctrine, violently attacks opponents? The difference is that the judge judges, punishing the culprit based on the law and due process of law. The militant, who also imagines that he is punishing the guilty, prejudges, and acts according to political beliefs and platforms, not according to the legal provisions and the courts. These, incidentally, can be deformed to fit the "method".

In Nazi doctrine, the Jews were guilty. Guilty of bringing blacks to Germany to weaken Aryan blood. And they were responsible for subjecting the country to a demeaning interest regime that hampered economic growth. This is what Hitler recorded in his pamphlet book, "Mein Kampf" (*My Fight*). The implicit message in the leader's speeches was that the Germans should ignore the courts and the laws and do "justice" with their own hands.

Even on the battlefield, two struggling armies can incorporate the "hate" factor into their action because it enhances the adrenaline rush and can hasten a solution. But hate is not the central element, because it even acts to disrupt discipline and obedience. The main impulses of battlefield action are the defense of the homeland (or of the cause), the need to refuse the invasion of one who can bring servitude, the belief in the superiority of his doctrine over that of the enemy, and, in more pathological cases, engaging in the project of saving the world with a supposedly wonderful doctrine by eliminating the opposites, characterized by the color of the flag or simply by ethnicity.

Coldness. How did Joseph Mengele see his Jewish patients?

When physician Joseph Mengele killed thousands of women and unborn children in his pseudo-eugenic experiments, he was driven not by some kind of hatred, but by pathological belief in a partisan doctrine. According to his statement, the Jewish patients in his hands were seen as objects, not as human beings. It is not hatred that feeds this kind of vision, but adherence to a cold ethnocentric campaign.

Therefore, in politics and war, we need to be careful about certain analyzes that mix personal feelings usually directed at close circles, whether family or professional life, with collective motivations at the national or international level. No matter how stupid or unjustified we find, warlike acts or political fanaticism are supported by method, not hate.

Chapter 3 - Traces

The great concern of the Yalta Conference, as well as the Paris Conference and the UN at the end of 1945, was to control Germany, which had been the center of World War I and rearmed for revenge, triggering World War II.

The East was as conflagrated as Europe in the years of World War II, but Japan's surrender seemed to have disarmed the spirits along the Pacific Ocean. The Korean region, which had been a colony of Japan for a few decades, was divided between North Korea, allied with the Soviet Union, and South Korea, allied with the United States.

There were, however, two major problems that were underestimated that year. Because of them, what came after World War II was not a period of total peace, but of various conflicts around the world, forming what was commonly called the Cold War.

The first of the two problems was the indefinite situation of Indochina (Vietnam). Colony of France, falling into the hands of the collaborationists and Free France again, served as the scenery of fights between Japan and the United States in the years of the conflict. Communist-minded Ho Chi-Min had proclaimed Vietnam's independence, but the world powers were unwilling to support him.

Stalin. What type of dictator has the most reading practice?

The second problem, easily foreseeable but not to the knowledge of the time: The Soviet Union, which fought in line with the Allied Forces to defeat Nazism, was a dictatorship.

Whether conservative, whether proletarian, dictatorships have only one purpose: Tutelage. The governed are no longer subjects or citizens and are seen as grown children. Before the Enlightenment, dictators, who we understand as tyrants, held power through the violence and fear it engendered. In the Contemporary Era, all kinds of dictators, from Haitian Pope Doc to Romanian Nikolai Ceausescu, also use fear, but their most powerful weapon is generosity to the poor. At the same time as they persecute and kill intellectuals and rebels, they sweeten the mouths of the poor with blessings. The big difference between the head of the conservative dictatorship and that of the "democratic dictatorship" (the term is from Lenin) is that this second reads a little more than the first. With more reading, the head of the "democratic dictatorship" uses more effective means to prevent hunger within the population.

At the beginning of the Russian Revolution Lenin's plan was to renew leadership. After his death, the position he held as chairman of the Council of People's Commissars was held successively by Aleksei Rykov (since February 1924), Viacheslav Molotov (since December 1930) and Iosif Stalin (since May 1941). As is well known, since 1924 Stalin, as secretary general of the Communist Party, had exercised full control of politics and government, making the office of chairman of the council decorative until his rise to office in 1941. Since then, he has become the absolute leader, de jure and de facto, of the Soviet Union, until his death in March 1953.

Korea. Who started the Korean War in 1950?

After the communist army of Mao Zedong, in October 1949, defeated the Chiang Kai-Shek government, causing it to flee to Taiwan, Chinese and North Koreans, with support from the Soviet Union, began planning a war leading to the incorporation of South Korea into North Korea. On June 25th, 1950, North Korean troops invaded South Korea, and on June 26th, the Korean War officially began, with combats taking place until July 27th, 1953, without never to be signed an armistice or an agreement to end the conflict. Everything went on as before, discounting deaths and material losses.

The number of Chinese dead is estimated at 2.5 million, in a total of 3 million casualties on both sides. By the number of casualties given the duration, the Korean War is considered the most violent conflict in human history.

How was postwar dissension possible if Russians and Americans were able to fight in a coordinated and strong alliance to destroy Nazism? As stated above, the impossibility of peaceful and lasting agreements was at the option of Russians, and, since 1949, Chinese, for the lifetime dictatorial form of the exercise of power.

Indochina. Which countries were French Indochina before?

Since the early twentieth century France had been keeping Indochina as a colony, in the territory where Laos, Cambodia, and Vietnam would later emerge. Under the Great Depression in 1929, France began to have serious problems in the region, facing independence movements.

Shortly after World War II, in 1946, the so-called Indochina War began between the rebel groups and France, lasting until 1954.

Cambodia declared its independence in 1945, and France recognized the act in 1949, but imposed several restrictions, deciding to dominate defense, diplomacy and other areas of power. Independence would, however, be granted "within the framework of the French union".

Vietnam's independence was declared, as we saw above, in 1944. Laos gained its independence in 1949, but was soon plunged into civil war that lasted several years. In 1945 India and Pakistan became independent from Britain and Indonesia declared independence from the Netherlands.

France resisted in Indochina until 1954, when, struggling with rebellions in Algeria, decided to abandon the East colony. At the Geneva Conference, the autonomy of the three resulting countries was established, but with the division of Vietnam into two, the pro-Soviet North and the pro-America South, which in practice split the region into four countries. It was decided that a year later there would be a plebiscite in both Vietnam, which would decide on unification or definitive separation.

At the scheduled time, North Vietnam held the consultation, but in South Vietnam the authorities struck a coup d'état, which prevented the referendum and determined that South Vietnam would remain a US ally. North Vietnamese soldiers then infiltrated the territory of South Vietnam promoting guerrillas to achieve unification.

Vietnam. What role did photographs play in the Vietnam War?

It was clear that South Vietnam would not sustain alone in the fight against the North Vietnam guerrillas, the so-called Viet Cong, for it was no secret that the Chinese and Soviets supported with men and resources the incorporation of South Vietnam from the north side.

The following year, 1955, the United States decided to give southern allied war support, thus starting the *Vietnam War*, or the Second Indochina War, which lasted until 1975. More than 4 million Vietnamese and neighbors died in this conflict. From the United States, more than 58,000 soldiers died, and 1,700 were reported missing.

It was two decades of war waged between great powers, but having as its stage a small country divided in two.

If South Korea survived, such a thing did not occur to South Vietnam. US troops withdrew in 1975, like French troops did in 1954.

The reasons for this retreat were various. One was, of course, the psychological and political wear and tear of such a lasting war.

The Three Causes of War

According to Sun Tzu, any country is heading for exhaustion when sustaining a protracted war of more than six months. The United States suffered no significant losses in the financial sector because the war was located in a small area. But successive casualties and a boycott campaign within the country led the government to conclude that continuing the war would mean acting contrary to the will of the population.

The Communist Party of the United States had popular support in the 2% range. Therefore, it was not the desire to help the Asian communists that was the engine of resistance to the conflict. In the majority's view, lifetime dictatorships were there, giving support to North Vietnam. So the war was theirs, not the Americans'.

Among many news materials, two photographs released by the press were fatal to the continuity of that conflict. The first of these was made by war reporter Eddie Adams, on February 1, 1968, and showed Colonel Nugunen Ngoc Loan executing a prisoner from North Vietnam. The photo later won the Pulitzer Prize and became a historic icon. What caught the eye was the way the act took place. The colonel was aiming at the prisoner's forehead, who was standing with his hands tied back, in a public square. In the other photo, taken on June 8th, 1972, by photographer Huynh Cong "Nick" Ut, a 9-year-old girl, Phan Thi Kim Phuc, was running naked after being hit by napalm, or "Agent Orange", a defoliant evacuated from helicopters to destroy the forest cover that hid Vietnamese soldiers. The girl had to get rid of the clothes that burned her body. She ran among other children, who were dressed, but all with horror, showing that they were shouting, and with armed soldiers walking behind them. Today Kim Phuc lives in Canada and works as a UN ambassador for peace. Nick Ut's photo also won the Pulitzer Prize.

The atomic bombs on Hiroshima and Hagasaki killed adults and children indiscriminately. When in the early hours of the morning of August 6th, 1945, pilot Paul Tibbets fired from his plane, Enola Gay (it was the name of Tibbets's mother), the first atomic bomb on Hiroshima, he saw the city below, but saw no children, not even adults, once they were sleeping. Nor did any photographer show the world in those days the state of the stricken children.

The 1972 photo showing the girl Kim Phuc's suffering brought to homes of the United States the reality of war camps, in which, however careful, it is not possible to protect elderly, sick, disabled and children from crossfire (as for the soldiers, it was always understood that they were made to fight, although most were sent to the battlefront against their will). Since that 1972 photo, the campaign against war has intensified, in schools, media, churches and even the military. In another three years, the two-decade war has been deactivated.

With the withdrawal of the US forces, the North Vietnamese army entered Saigon, then the capital of South Vietnam, unified the two countries and renamed the capital to Ho Chi Minh City, in honor of the independence patriarch, who had died in 1969.

Cuba. Did Stalinism survive Stalin?

The moment of greatest danger to the world during the Cold War did not occur, however, during a war, as it was in Korea and Vietnam, but in the process of a revolution. It was because of the Cuban Revolution during the so-called Pig Bay Crisis, of April, 1961, that the world was on the brink of a nuclear conflict of the kind described in the 1957 film *On The Beach*, directed by Nevil Shute, meaning there would be no life left on the Earth. At that time, not only the United States, but also the Soviet Union had an atomic weapons arsenal.

Fidel Castro was a young lawyer very famous and beloved in Cuba for being a baseball champion, the most appreciated sport in the country. On January 1, 1959, after many advances and setbacks, Castro descended the Sierra Maestra with his brother Raul, Argentine doctor Ernesto "Che" Guevara, expert snipers Juan Almeida and Camilo Cienfuegos and other seven companions to face the dictatorship by Fulgencio Batista. Knowing the population's support for Fidel Castro and his "Rebel Army", Batista fled to the Dominican Republic. Castro appointed as president Manuel Urrutia Lleó, who took office on the 3rd.

Both Fidel Castro and Che Guevara were well received in the United States on different occasions. The first was to explain the revolution. The second, as Minister of Economy, was trying to negotiate resources for the new government.

From January 1, 1959, until early 1961, the revolution was considered a liberal movement, striving to set up a democratic regime in Cuba, in accordance with the rule of law.

Still in 1959 the government implemented an agrarian reform and eliminated the mafia. While seeking to do its best for Cuba, the government organized a conference with leading European intellectuals, who would show the most appropriate routes for the revolution. The best-known name among them was Jean-Paul Sartre, but there were others who were members of communist parties in their countries. The result was the recommendation that Cubans should align with the Soviet

Union, not the United States. Following this, Che Guevara made a long trip to Czechoslovakia, the Soviet Union and other Eastern European countries to enter into trade agreements.

On January 3rd, 1961, President Eisenhower, of the United States, broke diplomatic relations with Cuba. The world understood there that the Cuban balance had tipped to the Soviet Union, rejecting political and economic adherence to the United States.

By the time John Fitzgerald Kennedy took office as President, weeks later, the state of US-Cuba relations was already deteriorating.

In this spirit, the Bay of Pigs Invasion occurred between April 15th and 19th, 1961. Exiled Cubans decided to carry out this invasion in order to overthrow the new government, with immediate US support and subsequent recognition. of the Organization of American States (OAS).

The plan provided for the dominance of some area or city, where a provisional government would be installed. From there would be launched guerrilla groups which, later on, receiving US supporters, would overthrow the government.

Last-minute formed regiments joined Cuba's regular forces and easily repelled the rebel offensive. Several hundred invaders were killed and 1,189 of them were taken prisoner. Those who were identified as former Batista army officers were sentenced to death.

Attorney Robert Kennedy, brother of the president of the United States, after receiving exiles battered by defeat, decided to help Cuban exiles in planning a second invasion. Nicaraguan dictator Anastacio Somoza obtained authorization to use the territory of his country as a base for attack. Many camps were set up there and several attacks were launched against Cuba. The actions transcended the phase of the Bay of Pigs Invasion and the ensuing Missile Crisis, as it was only terminated when the exiles mistakenly attacked the Spanish ship Sierra Aranzazu, confusing it with a Cuban ship. In the attack were killed the captain and two crew. The United States government has compensated Spain and closed the camps in Nicaragua.

Amid clashes between exiles and the new Cuban government, US forces discovered on October 15th 1962, an arsenal of Moscow atomic weapons installed on the island. From the 15th to the 28th, the so-called Missile Crisis, which in Cuba is called the October Crisis, took place. The US government has deemed it inadmissible the installation of this Soviet missile base in such an area só near the United States. John Kennedy demanded that Soviet leader Nikita Khrushchev withdrew these weapons.

The negotiations were very tense and the world was apprehensive as events unfolded. At no other time in the Cold War was a nuclear conflict between the two major world powers of those days so close at hand.

Khrushchev finally relented and the withdrawal was completed on October 28th. After failed attempts by exiles fighting Fidel Castro with US aid, that was a great victory against the Soviet side.

Kennedy, however, could not celebrate. Stalin died a decade earlier, but Stalinism was very much alive.

Kennedy. In what eastern capital did Lee Oswald reside?

On November 22nd, 1963, President John F. Kennedy and his wife Jacqueline were driving in an open car during an official visit to the city of Dallas, Texas, when he was shot in the head. A few minutes after the fatal shot, the killer, who acted from the window of a building, was arrested. He was former Louisiana marine Lee Harvey Oswald, 24, who flatly denied being the perpetrator of the murder.

Two days after the president's death, Lee Oswald, while being transported for questioning, was shot and killed by Jack Leon Ruby, a Dallas night manager.

In 1994 another former military man, James Files, came out, stating that he, not Oswald, was the actual author of the shooting that killed the president. However, post-revelation investigations found many inconsistencies in Files' stories, and he was put aside.

Oswald was born in New Orleans two months after his father, Robert Edward Lee Oswald, died of a stroke, so his mother raised him with the help of his older brother.

When he was 14 years old, he got into a fight with stepbrother John Pic and was diagnosed with a schizoid personality with aggressive tendencies by a city psychiatrist.

At 17 he joined the Armed Forces and some said it was a way of getting out of control of his overprotective mother.

Among the Marines, he went through several episodes of assaults on his companions and suffered punishment. In 1959 he traveled by ship to Finland and from there defected to the Soviet Union. He returned to the United States only in 1962, accompanied by his daughter and wife, Maria Prussakova, whom he met in Minsk, capital of Belarus. She was the daughter of a KGB colonel, the regime's political police.

He settled in Dallas and was soon in trouble, such as the attempt to assassinate General Walker, a very conservative military man. Oswald fled to Mexico and at the Cuban embassy sought a visa to return to the Soviet Union.

On the day of the presidential tragedy, Kennedy was in a convertible car ride on Dealey Square, in front of the building where Oswald worked, the *Texas School Book Depository*. The entourage heard three shots, and the second, or more likely the third, hit the head of the chief of State.

Police Officer Marrion Baker of the Dallas City Police noticed that gunfire came from that building and immediately he climbed the stairs and saw Lee Oswald walking fast at the cafeteria, on the second floor. Baker gave a voice of arrest, detaining Oswald. But soon the chief of staff of the house, Roy Trully, came and testified that Oswald was a local employee. Oswald was then left alone and soon headed for his residence.

Aware of the incident, law enforcement officials understood that Oswald was the number one suspect, and the search began. When he was found, at the Texas Theater, he killed police officer J. D. Tippit, who had arrested him at that time. The other police officers had already convinced him that this was the man who murdered the president.

Returning to Washington, and already sworn in as president, Lindon Johnson installed the Warren Commission to handle the case investigation. There were seven members under the leadership of the Supreme Court President, Earl Warren. The others were Allen Dulles, Gerald Ford, John McCloy, John Sherman Cooper, Richard Russell, and Thomas Boggs.

The conclusion of the Warren Commission was that Oswald was the real killer, but many doubt that. The fact that the suspect was killed two days later while being transferred for questioning has left a cloud of skepticism that continues to this day, fueling countless conspiracy theories.

The point which the Warren Commission most wanted to clarify remained inconclusive: Did Oswald act under the express orders of any organization, or did the act of his own accord, acting on his own, like a terrorist on the line of what are today called "lone wolves"?

Having resided in the Soviet Union and being the son-in-law of a KGB agent, there was little to speculate about his motives. Under external orders or not, he was part of a doctrinal network.

The "lone wolf", by the way, does not receive orders from a central organization, from where he is called "lone", but receives inflows from what we may call "diffuse order". He acts from the perspective of fulfilling the will of the messianic leader. Just as no thread was found linking Kennedy's murder to Khrushchev's office, nor did one find a direct link between Stalin and the murder of his rival Trotsky, in Mexico, at the hands of Ramon Mercader, or a communication route between the anachronic caliph.of the Islamic State (ISIS), Abou Bakr, and the massacre of the Charlie Hebdo journalists (01/07/2015) and, later, the Bataclan Concert Hall (11/13/2015). This was a religious leader deformed by fanaticism, but the fact that the messianic leader calls himself anti-religious, when appropriate, does not exempt him from the classification of messianic. A messianic leader is not a dead man, but a living chief who directly or indirectly commands a legion of followers capable of killing and dying for him.

Deposition. How many coups occurred in Brazil in April 1964?

The response to the most daring Cold War act related to a chief of State, which was the death of Kennedy, came without a detailed plan, but it was not long in coming, and this was the installation of conservative dictatorships as a counterpoint to dictatorships commanded by the Russian Revolution, allegedly defending the interests of the proletariat.

John F. Kennedy had a friendly and trusting relationship with Brazilian President Joao Goulart. When his brother-in-law, Leonel Brizola, governor of the State of Rio Grande do Sul, expropriated US subsidiary IT&T, Kennedy was able to count on Goulart, who used federal funds to indemnify the headquarters of that multinational company.

However, to Goulart's misfortune, inflation that had been growing exponentially since the Kubitschek administration (1956-1961) entered a phase of intense acceleration. The president lost support day after day, suffering various kinds of accusations, including that he intended to hand over the country to the Communists, until the Federal Senate table decided to strike a coup d'état, on April 1, 1964, declaring in vacancy the position of President of the Republic, taking advantage of a presidential trip to Rio Grande do Sul. The chief minister of the Civil House, Darcy Ribeiro, sent a statement to Parliament notifying about the trip, but the Senate kept reading that the chief of State had left the country without the necessary notice to the National Congress.

The following day the Brazilian Congress inaugurated as president of the Republic Pascoal Ranieri Mazzilli, President of the Chamber of Deputies, but he only lasted 14 days in office. On the 7th, the governor of Guanabara, a state that was only the city of Rio de Janeiro, called several governors to his palace, those who supported the coup, and proposed to exchange Mazzilli for a general. The name of Marshal Castello Branco was taken to the National Congress, registered as a candidate on the 9th and elected by parliamentarians on the 11th. General Juarez Tavora submitted his own candidacy, but was virtually ignored. On the 15th the National Congress inaugurated the new president. Unlike the 1930 Revolution, in which the military gave the October 3rd coup and called a civilian to preside over the country, in 1964 the civilians delivered the April 1 coup and called the military to head the state.

There were two coups d'état in the same fortnight. First, Goulart was removed from office on the grounds that he had fled the country. But he only flew to Uruguay on the 2nd, after the inauguration of Mazzilli. Second, the president, under the Constitution, would be Mazzilli, and the National Congress had no mandate to hold a presidential election the following week, defenestrating him by recourse to the fait accompli, but it did só, swearing in a military man who until the end of the previous month was in line with the current called "legalistic".

Dictatorships

Although it continued to adopt undemocratic measures, such as the elimination of political parties, the suspension of elections and the annulment of elective terms, the military government had the support of the market and the mainstream press, as the economy remained in the liberal-privatist field and the inflation was being reduced. In 1968, inspired by French university students, Brazilian students and leftist leaders rose against the government. In addition to street demonstrations there were kidnappings, explosions and clashes. On December 13th Marshal Artur da Costa e Silva, then president, signed Institutional Act No. 5 (AI-5), giving the chief of State discretion over the Constitution. The dictatorship was installed under suitably biased legal paints.

The support the military regime received from the population was due to the attack on inflation, but the generals used the power that conservative leaders gave them to persecute the allies of the Soviet Union. If a man trained in the eastern country could kill the president of the western leader, no US ally was safe. To have the slightest guarantee of their physical integrity, presidents of states not supported by the Stalinist East had to hunt, arrest, and kill Communists.

Spread. Have military dictatorships become isolated cases? The idealistic youth began to act, under reverse effect, against the military. Those who turned out to be communists or supporters of the Soviet Union were candidates for physical disappearance. Old politicians linked to the left were banned from the country.

The reading of the events of the Cold War of the early 1960s by the Brazilian military was shared by the Armed Forces of many dozens of countries. If before the Brazilian military regime military dictatorships were isolated cases around the world, after 1964 this became the fashion.

Bolivia-64. On November 2nd, 1964, Aviation General René Barrientos Ortuño delivered a coup d'état in Bolivia, toppling President Víctor Paz Estenssoro.

Algeria-65. On June 19th, 1965, the military Houari Boumediéne gave a coup d'état, toppling the first Algerian president, Ahmed Ben Bella.

Congo-65. Lieutenant General Mobutu Sese Seko overthrew President Joseph Kasa-Vubu, whom he protected and apparently supported, on November 24th, 1965. In 1971 he changed the name of Congo to Zaire. After his death in 1997, from prostate cancer, authorities returned the former name to the country, calling it the Democratic Republic of Congo.

Argentina-66. In Argentina, on June 28th, 1966, a coup d'état led by General Juan Carlos Onganía overthrew President Arturo Illia, who was succeeded in 1970 by General Roberto Marcelo Levingston, who in 1971 replaced General Alejandro Agustín Lanusse, presidente until 1973. That year the country elected as president the union leader Hector Campora, who, as he had promised, made the old dictator General Juan Domingos Perón elected. The general, dying shortly thereafter, was succeeded by his wife Isabelita, who was overthrown by a new coup d'état in 1976, led by General Jorge Rafael Videla.

Indonesia-67. General Haji Mohammad Suharto delivered a coup d'état on February 22nd, 1967, against the first president of Indonesian Republican history, Makam Sukarno, remaining in power until May 1998.

Greece-67. On April 21st, 1967, Colonel Georgios Papadopoulos led a coup d'état against King Constantine II of Greece, installing the dictatorship of the colonels, while establishing Georgios Zoitakis as regent. In March, 1972, Papadopoulos himself became regent and, in May, 1973, President of the Republic.

Peru-68. In Peru, the October 3rd, 1968, coup d'état elevated General Juan Velasco Alvarado to the presidency. The dictatorship there maintained the respect for much of civil liberties, prompting the press to nickname the regime's generals as "muddy youths".

Libya-69. The coup in Libya was dealt with by Colonel Muamar al-Gaddafi, on September 1, 1969, which overthrew King Idris I, who was vested in office in 1951 by the UN General Assembly.

Uganda-71. President Milton Obote had traveled abroad when General Idi Amin Dada led a coup in Uganda, ousting him on January 25th, 1971. One of the cruelest dictatorships of that decade followed.

Korea-72. In South Korea, General Park Chung-hee had been democratically elected in 1963, but accompanying the authoritarian winds of the following years, he issued a discretionary constitution along the lines of Brazil's Institutional Act No. 5 and initiated the so-called Fourth Republic, on October 17th, 1972.

Chile-73. Highly emblematic of that phase, due to its degree of violence, was the coup of General Augusto Pinochet against the government of President Salvador Allende, Chile, on September 11th, 1973.

Argentina-76. As stated above, Argentina suffered a new military coup in a matter of years, this time led by General Jorge Rafael Videla and destined to follow in the footsteps of Brazil's military regime, with bounded mandates among the military in command and brutal persecution of the Soviet Union supporters.

El-Salvador-77. In El Salvador it was Colonel Carlos Humberto Romero who delivered the coup d'état on July 1, 1977.

Turkey-80. On November 12th, 1980, it was Turkey's turn, which suffered a coup d'état led by General Kenen Evren.

Egypt-81. In the case of Egypt, the president, who was Anwar al-Sadat, was killed by his soldiers on October 6th, 1981, during a military parade. A week later, Aviator-General Hosni Mubarak took office as president, ruling until his overthrow in 2011.

Guatemala-82. On March 23rd, 1982, General Efraín Rios Montt overthrew Guatemalan President Fernando Romeo Lucas-García and installed a dictatorship, but was replaced in 1983 by General Oscar Humberto Mejía Víctores.

Guinea-84. On April 3rd, 1984, Colonel Lansana Conté began a bloodless coup in Guinea. Two days later he took office as president.

Defrosting

In those days of the 1980s the Soviet Union was moving towards what was later called Restructuring (*Perestroika*, in Russian). Although Nikita Khrushchev rose to the top while denouncing Stalin's crimes, the regime's authoritarianism remained vigorous, with both Krushev and his successor Leonid Brezhnev. In 1982, with the death of Brezhnev, the secretary general of the Communist Party, who since Stalin's time had been the de facto chief of the Soviet dictatorship, happened to be Yuri Andrópov, a refined man, even though he was leader of the KGB, and he showed, supported by Prime Minister Nikolai Tikhonov (1980-1985), who did not share the practice of installing life leaders. After his brief stint in the post, he was succeeded, after his death on February 13th, 1984, by Konstantin Tchernenko, who died on March 10th of the following year, and was succeeded by lawyer Mikhail Gorbachev.

In Brazil, after the Opposition Party, the Brazilian Democratic Movement (MDB), won the parliamentary elections of late 1974, defeating the party that supported the military government, the National Renewing Alliance (Arena), the President of the Republic, General Ernesto Geisel, announced the "slow, safe and gradual" policy of Distension. There would be the political openness, as demanded by the MDB, but the pace and breadth would be dictated by the regime. The AI-5 (Institutional Act No. 5), for example, was not revoked until October 13th, 1978. In Brazil, as in all military dictatorships outside the influence of Eastern Europe, the fear of the Soviet Union remained virtually intact.

In 1980, with the entry of Nikolai Tikhonov as prime minister of the Soviet Union, the Stalinist dictatorship finally began to show signs of exhaustion. With the death of Leonid Brezhnev in 1982 the fate of the Soviet Union lurched. Slight winds of political openness began to blow in Moscow.

President Ernesto Geisel, fulfilling the barracks' desire, said in a speech that his successor would still be a general. "Brazil still needs a military man", he said. In March, 1979, General Joao Baptista de Oliveira Figueiredo took office as president.

President Geisel, who in 1977 had to counter a "hard-line" coup attempt led by General Sylvio Frota, opposed to the Distension, had no way of guessing what would be his successor's government, on the contrary, he would have delivered already in 1979 power to civilian hands.

The annual inflation at that time was estimated at 40%. President Figueiredo, who demanded before the inauguration of the traditional five-year term to six years, ended his period in 1985 facing annual inflation of 240%, even though he reintroduced economist Antonio Delfim Netto, who at one time, under the General Medici's government, from the early 1970s, had done a good job of reducing the inflation rate. Under Figueiredo, he had no success.

What was once a dreaded dictatorship, mainly because of the AI-5, under General Figueiredo has become a ridiculous regime.

Worldwide, the military dictatorships dissolved, discovering that they had no reason to exist anymore. The Cold War had reached the downward curve of its life cycle.

Built in August, 1961, to prevent Germans from the eastern part of the city, under Soviet influence, to continue migrating to the western part, allied with the United States, the Berlin Wall was a symbol of the political division of the world between enthusiasts of the market economy and the planned economy. Under the meltdown in relations, begun with the administration that settled in Moscow in 1980, which in some way had to do with President Richard Nixon's US visit to China in 1973, it was a matter of semesters or years the change in the way of living between the two types of government conception. The overthrow of the symbol, that is, the fall of the Berlin Wall, took place on November 9th, 1989, with the Soviet Union living under the leadership of Gorbachev.

Chapter 4 - Causes

With the fall of the Wall in 1989, Professor Francis Fukuyama, of the Stanford University, California, risked a world-wide guess: the concept of *End of History*. The tension between East and West would be definitively alleviated, given that the great reason for the conflicts over the last decades rested on the difference in conception of economic management: the Soviets and Chinese cultivated the philosophy of planned economy, while Western Europeans and Americans keeping defending the continuity of the market economy.

History. Como se deu a queda do Xá Rehza Parlevi?

Fukuyama did not take into account, or at least fail to see with due weight, a historical fact that occurred in the year before the beginning of the Tiknonov administration in the Soviet Union. On January 16th, 1979, the Persian Shah Rehza Pahlevi was stripped of his throne and exiled by popular pressure, which united civil and religious sectors against the monarchy. On February 11th, the office of the "provisional government", which still ruled the country in line with the deposed chief of State, was dissolved. Formed as a new government, said revolutionary, it was repealed the banning decree of the country's largest religious leader, Ayatollah Ruhollar Khomeini, who was in exile in Paris. He returned to Persia, with the support of the Communist Party of the country and all the forces opposing the shah, who was living in Egypt, until his death a few months later. On April 1, it occurred the transformation of the country into theocratic republic, a *contradictio in termis*. In December, Khomeini became "Guide of the Revolution", the de facto monarch. The country gained a new name: *Islamic Republic of Iran*.

What Fukuyama despised in his analysis was the fact that almost all the wars in human history until the nineteenth century had religious differences as their main engine, although almost always some more justifiable subterfuge was used, such as honor, market or throne. .

We had not reached the End of History, because the theocracy, which seemed buried in the rubble of papal States, extinguished by Italian unification, and the Buddhist Tibet, which China dismantled, still held great resurgence potential. Nobody who tried to refute Fukuyama's ideas at the time raised the argument for the return of Islamic power as a counterexample. It seemed almost as harmless as a Jehovah's Witness community, which repudiates the existence of armies.

Pseudo-secularism

The positivism of Auguste Comte, a more comprehensive and detailed rereading of Saint-Simon's industrialism, of whom Comte was secretary in his youth, built a political proposal that rejected Democracy, Jurisprudence, and Psychology. Industrialists, technicians, and intellectuals would govern the countries through the system he called "sociocracy", declaredly a dictatorship: "Chief indicates his successor". Since no term was set for a mandate, it was assumed that the chief would choose someone to succeed him after death.

The artisans of the "scientific socialism", the basis of the political doctrine that inspired both the Russian Revolution and the creation of the Soviet Union, also used ideas from Saint-Simon, along with proposals and experiences from Robert Owen, Pierre-Joseph Proudhon, Charles Fourier and Etienne Cabet, among others. Their set of political proposals has been called "Utopian socialism", as opposed to the novelty presented by philosophers of the historical materialism.

Scorning and ridiculing the Comtist positivism, the historical materialism adopted the same rejection of Jurisprudence, called bourgeois law, or "their law"; Democracy, which would not be replaced by the dictatorship of sociocracy, but by the "dictatorship of the proletariat"; and Psychology, a science completely neglected in the writings of the "scientific socialism" in the nineteenth century. The positive point of the proposal is that its authors recommended that it should be applied first in the most industrially developed centers, as was England at the time. No Russia. However, it was not possible to construct a process that could convince the British people to exchange their "bourgeois democracy" for a dictatorship, even though it was the "dictatorship of the proletariat", which meant "majority" dictatorship.

Implanted the dictatorship of the proletariat in Russia, years later John Maynard Keynes wrote that the Soviets followed their scientific book as if it were a Bible. Iosif Stalin, who emerged as a great leader after Vladimir Lenin's death, was a former Georgia seminarian. Unlike Lenin, he ordered the burning of Orthodox Catholic churches as a means of eliminating resistance to his regime. The idea was to preserve only subservient clerics.

Called the "genius guide of the peoples", Stalin pontificated for decades as a savior of the world to millions of militants. He was a messiah of a secular religion.

It was part of Comte's positivist doctrine that he should not investigate first and final causes. This had no solution, nor did it matter for the purpose of that philosophy. However, at his maturity Comte got a girlfriend, Clotilde de Vaux, who was a very religious woman. She convinced him of a fact of crystal clear understanding for most people: most need religion, and can't live without it.

Comte, while realizing that the word "religion" derives from the verb "to *religare*" (to rewire), but without accepting to give in to transcendentalism, created the "positivist religion", or the "religion of humanity". Instead of a deity, the altar would have a statue of a woman (Clotilde, of course), holding a child in her arms. This statue represented humanity. In place of apostles or saints, the sides of the Positivist Church would bear statues of past scientists and philosophers. For the functioning of this church the philosopher wrote a book called the Positivist Catechism.

The secular religion was therefore codified.

Twentieth-century political leaders did not explicitly embrace the positivist religion. But it underlies the behavior of most of them, especially those who implanted dictatorships.

World War II kamikazes died on a suicide mission in the name of the emperor, who was regarded as a transcendent god. It is not difficult to realize that, for the one who is leaving life, dying for a supposedly divine cause is more comfortable than dying for a political cause constituted as a secular religion, a "religion of humanity". For Lee Oswald, his death must have been far more foolish than the death of the Cathar fanatics, the Gnostic followers of Mary Magdalene, killed at the furnace under Simon de Montfort, Baron of Amury, in the early 13th century. They reportedly went to the campfire singing hymns, praising the Lord for the grace of being delivered from the prison of their flesh.

In the end, religion never left the scene in the war environment. When it was imagined, throughout the twentieth century, that the administrations of countries had separated religion from the State, secular religion contaminated people's brains.

What happened in 1979 in the Persian Gulf was that religion returned to participate in politics and wars following medieval molds. That which the French Revolution buried, at ground level, Tehran exhumed.

Materialism. Has the academic materialism given importance to inflation?

Historical materialism would be the key to human behavior if people acted like irrational animals. Pavlov's dogs and Skinner's pigeons responded to alimentary stimuli mechanically. Everything was predictable. Historical materialism very well explains the purely animal side of human social actions. Beyond this limit one has the question of the "ventriolesque interpretation of history", as Antonio Gramsci, founder of the now-defunct Italian Communist Party, jockingly said.

Behavioral materialism was developed by Reverend Thomas Robert Malthus, history's first professor of Economics. From his book "Essay on Population" historical materialism was derived by intellectuals who mocked his proposals. Malthus inspired Charles Darwin in developing the theory of natural selection precisely by the material aspect of behavior. Caught by periods of severe scarcity, the Chinese began eating locusts and other insects, Malthus explained. If we continued to promote population growth in a disorderly manner, we would have serious problems ahead in the face of the food dispute, and now we also know about drinking water. Darwin recognized Malthus's contribution to his work, without any fear of being diminished by it.

Albert Einstein, advocate of democratic socialism, not the dictatorship of the proletariat, knew that humanity acted for dictates superior to those of behavioral materialism. That is why, at the end of World War II, he called on the great powers to first avoid the nuclear race and, secondly, to found a world government, having as its principal partners the United States and the Soviet Union, resulting from there the creation of the UN, which got out of the paper three months after the publication of the scientist's manifesto.

Texts of historical materialism predicted in the mid-1890s that a world war would soon occur, because the great powers, including the British Empire, the Austro-Hungarian Empire, the Russian Empire, and the German Empire, were disputing the world market, and they could not come to a peaceful solution. They got it right, but the spark that ignited the gunpowder barrel was not the market dispute itself, but the inflation of the Austro-Hungarian Empire, which oppressed the Balkans and led anarchist groups to carry out armed attacks against authorities. Materialism is a valid tool of analysis, but it is not a cause and effect mechanism for human behavior in that it goes beyond its purely animal scope.

The human mass tolerates tyrannical oppressions in almost every way, but reacts indignantly against price increases and tax increases. It is very worrying that historians, psychologists and other scholars pay little attention to the role of inflation, or dearness, in social upheavals. Inflation does not mean just taking food off another's table, but doing so and much more by manipulating a cultural symbol, which is the currency. Without the use of Psychology, as it was recommended by Stuart Mill, the main point of the course of history is ignored. Obviously, this is much more complex than the mere calculation of the transfer of material goods from one person to another.

Leaders

In addition to the force that inflation has in driving the great changes of history, as in the French Revolution, the other aspect that is neglected, or at least ceases to have the look it deserves, is that of the influence of persuasive leadership on masses, as was the case with Hitler, but also many others before him. Of course, Hitler was able to reach the unwary citizen's ear directly over the radio, while earlier leaders, from Guttenberg, relied on the formation of other leaders through newspapers and magazines, only then to reach the most humble and poorly literate worker. This interface, reading, provided debugging, so rising leaders would have to show some intellectual ability above what the average person possessed. The strong, low-minded, influential leaders who, like Hitler, depended on ear-to-ear conversation, were able to form very localized and restricted armies of the faithful.

In times of radio, TV, and now the Internet, which is the cheap TV, the persuasive power of oligophrenic leaders reaches previously unimaginable levels. As David Ricardo and Marshall McLuhan clearly saw, a machine always greatly extends the reach of its owner.

In addition to Hitler, the twentieth century met the great mesmerizing force of Iosif Stalin, Benito Mussolini (self-styled "apostle of violence"), Hideki Tojo, Francisco Franco, Pol Pot, Jiang Qing (Mao Zedong's widow), Idi Amin, Haji Suharto, Slobodan Milosevic and Saddam Hussein, among many others.

There were also those leaders who, without reaching the leadership of a State or government, dominated the minds of a flock of people, including people with intelligence far superior to the individual who became the center of the "cause". A case of great richness of data for psychological studies is that of the mediocre musician Charles Manson, a mystical leader who went to Los Angeles to create a community of artists and admirers who followed his orders. Many murders were committed at the behest of the leader, who thought he was able to mislead the police, which, in his assessment, would soon blame the "Black Panthers" group. The case gained international notoriety when one of the murdered people was actress Sharon Tate, wife of film director Roman Polanski.

Among the notorious delinquent leaders perhaps the most significant name is Al Capone. He arrived in New York as a child and in adulthood surrendered to crime. He took advantage of Prohibition to traffic alcohol and made a huge fortune, becoming the largest acting mafia boss in the United States. Arrested for inconsistency in the tax return, served time in Alcatraz prison. When he was released in 1939 he was mentally damaged, in an irreversible state. The second most important name in the mafia is Charlie "Lucky" Luciano, who got rich by controlling heroin trafficking in New York. He had mastery over gambling and prostitution. He was also part of the distilled alcohol trafficking during Prohibition. He returned to Italy and continued his criminal empire there, dying of heart failure in Naples in January 1962. He is considered the father of the modern organized crime. Other prominent mobster bosses were Frank Costello and Carlo Gambino.

Outside the Sicilian mafia, the most emblematic case of criminal leadership was that of Colombian drug trafficker Pablo Escobar, murdered on December 2nd, 1993, in the city of Medellin.

Unlike political leaders, who have to act openly in search of followers from all the social levels, crime leaders are able to control niches. More powerful criminals run networks of obedient criminals. If the leader does not have great influence, then he is denounced. If he has the proper power of mind domination, he gets a hoop of protection from his followers.

A genocide can have one or more exterminating agents under his command, without the leader personally being involved in deaths. Josef Mengele, for example, was a cold killer under Hitler's rule, committing thousands of murders just within his medical activity. Fled from Germany after the war, he was welcomed with guarantees by the regime of General Juan Domingos Perón, Argentina, among other Nazi refugees, and moved to Brazil when the winds changed color in the southern country. Living with a false identity, he died in the beach town of Bertioga, Sao Paulo, in February 1979.

In addition to the audience gap between the political leader and the criminal leader, open the first, closed the latter, the other major difference is that the troubled political leader proves disastrous to the masses only when he has already succeeded, while the boss of crime has to emerge as a delinquent in the early stages of his career. A promising dictator in his career is, as stated above, someone who tutors and apparently protects the poor, while persecuting and massacring the intellectuals. Thus, while the government does not crumble by its own incompetence, or by factors unrelated to personal will, the opposition cannot win the trust of the masses.

As regards the character, both are of the same nature. For such a leader, practicing or commanding genocide is in his field of perspective, as a means of achieving his goals, either in the name of his "famiglia", the group of comrades, or in the name of the national fraction he is keen to represent.

Both the formation of an "empire" in organized crime and the consolidation of an authoritarian populist government require some years of work. When Hitler won in 88 percent the self-nomination plebiscite, in 1934, by abolishing parliamentarism, he showed that he had the backing of the near totality of the German electorate. But at that time, with only one year in office, the Germans would not be ready to die for him if there was a summons to do so. From 1939, as it turned out, he had already conquered hearts and minds. The population was already willing to kill and die for its leader.

Term. Is term limit sound for the population?

In the Republic, however, no sensible ruler seeks to be reelected for too many terms. Under a parliamentary regime, the chief of State should not exceed four or five years. Reelection, which leads the commander in chief to remain for eight, ten or twelve years in office, is a measure of the most reckless in politics.

If the president, by law, exercises only a four-year or five-year term, the premier may be reelected once or twice, with 12 years being a reasonable limit, but eight years being more recommended. The mental health of the governed is assured by the ban on the reelection of the chief of State.

Initially, the idea of limiting the number of years of the supreme chief's term is a matter of liberal politicians, not of an academic outcome. Conservatives and their plebiscitary antipodes see no problem keeping the commander in chief for decades in office. Democratic politicians, trying to put themselves in the middle ground, try one model or another, without a clear bias towards the long-lived side or the alternate side.

As in the last decades the world has lived with both types of leadership, the academy already has enough comparative data to conclude by abandoning the idea of the long-term presidency.

Let us compare, for example, the management of Luigi Einaudi, second president of the Republic of Italy, who served for seven years, from 1948 to 1955, with the management of any president who has been held in office for more than twice that period. Anyone who finds one who has not plunged his country into wars, revolutions, or a miserable state of misery, will face a leader with a weak personality, who does not impress his comrades. Some long-term presidents were Jose Eduardo dos Santos (Angola, 1979-2017, 18 years), Robert Mugabe (Zimbabwe, 1980-2017, 37 years), Omar al-Bashir (Sudan, 1989-2019, 30 years), Hosni Mubárak (Egypt, 1981-2011, 30 years), Alfredo Stroessner (Paraguay, 1954-1989, 35 years), Hafez al-Assad (Syria, 1971-2000, 29 years), François Duvalier "Papa Doc" (Haiti, 1957-1971, 14 years), Haji Suharto (Indonesia, 1967-1998, 31 years).

On the side of the governed, the harms of the president's longevity are innumerable, but the position gives great gains to him, who, if not well informed about the danger that his stay beyond reasonable represents, will seek to convince the commanded that the the best option to head the country in the coming years is himself.

But he does not realize the negative transformation around him in relation to himself: from the sixth or seventh year of his term, his mind is deciphered by his acolytes, his trusted men. The power he held in the beginning because of his personal magnetism disappears. From then on his authority is artificial, all grounded in the meaning of the office. If he is an individual of violent character, he will tend to physically eliminate old allies who are already untrustworthy. If he is a quiet person, or if the laws prevent him from resorting to truculent methods, he will continue to command, because the position gives him that right, but he will only be a player whose bids are all mapped, allowing not only children, but also adults, see that "the king is naked".

Re-election. Competent leader needs long term?

As much as the satisfaction of being at the top of Maslow's pyramid is something that delights almost every citizen, staying in that position for eight, nine, or more years makes the individual a ridiculous puppet, even when given to violent acts. And that sentiment will be greater to the extent that the republican conscience of his comrades is more pronounced.

If this president, seated in the presidential chair, considers himself to be respectful of democratic principles, then he must be aware of the concept of "contradiction of democracy".

According to Karl Mannheim, the contradiction of democracy is a phenomenon observed at the end of a poll. When citizens come together to choose the boss, they are all theoretically equal. Nobody disagrees that democracy depends on this condition. The moment the votes are cast, one of those citizens ceases to be the same as the others. He is the one who was elected. Now let us suppose these same citizens meet again after four years, for a new election, and among the candidates they see the one who was elected previously and wielded power for that quadrennium. He is running, like the others, but he is not an equal. He competes as a privileged boss, even if there has been a prior period of untying from office.

Candidates for reelection for leadership in democratic countries know that their application differs from that of newcomers, but they justify their decision to run by claiming the right to be judged on the term that ends. The alleged election becomes a plebiscite: the current boss remains, or not.

John Kenneth Galbraith advocated a ban on reelection for parliamentary office because, he explained, the first term was for voters, but the next served for "planning," that is, bureaucracy. The economist's reasoning was not very convincing. A congressman staying for three or four quadrennia in the same legislative house is no harm, except for novice competitors who want to take their place.

The experience one gained over the years makes the parliamentarian more competent and wiser. Winston Churchill was elected parliamentary for the first time at the age of 25, being reelected several times, leaving the House for a few years after the first election. Four decades later, at the age of 65, on May 10th, 1940, he became prime minister for the first time and reversed the British government's understanding about the Hitler's dictatorship. Contrary to what many imagine, few saw the destructive meaning of Nazism. Marshal Pétain agreed to form the collaborationist government in France because he saw Hitlerism as a very favorable novelty for the peoples. Without the election of Churchill, a seasoned parliamentarian, the Nazi disaster could have taken root in Europe and lasted for decades, with increasing expansion.

It may therefore be appropriate to limit the number of seats in the same house to 16 or 20 years, for example, without preventing parliamentarians from running for other parliaments. In a federation, the congressman of many terms may run for state assembly, and vice versa.

Parliamentarians, like other politicians, are the society's entourage scouts, along with the Armed Forces and diplomats. Your performance should be more valued. In times of tyranny, rulers were bandits who won a prize for conquering power, as they were hidden in caves and hunted at a far greater risk. In the age of developing democracy, honest, well-educated people who accept governing should be the object of admiration on the part of the voter. However, if they fight tooth and nail to get to the post, they give off a nasty signal, because, according to Plato, the self-candidate for government has no merit to govern.

If we need to limit terms of the chief of State, it is by categorical imperative: reelections and longevity of the President of the Republic lead to death.

Franklin Delano Roosevelt was president from 1933 to 1945, obtaining successive reelections. The number of reelections for president of the United States was unlimited at that time, for pure innocence, one might say. With the experience of World War II and analysis of its causes, it became clear to the country's politicians that the chief of State's longevity was a factory of gunpowder barrels. The greatest villain of the war took over the position of federal president of Germany with the intention of not leaving there while he lived, and was not the only tragic example in this regard. Stalin, who helped overthrow Nazism and then sustained the Cold War against the United States and all market economy countries, followed Hitler's purpose and left the post of main chief with only the last breath. In the United States, holders of presidential mandates, which are quadrennial terms, are now entitled to run for just one more election, so that a US president can run the country for a maximum of eight years.

As a burden for longevity, after the seventh year the president is seen as a "lame duck", someone with declining power and little effectiveness.

The ideal, however, is that there is no presidential reelection, because a four-year term, if it is short for an incompetent person, it is too long for someone with some ability. And the incompetent should not have a chance to reach this post.

Setback. Is China at risk under unlimited presidential terms?

After the fall of the Berlin Wall under Gorbachev and the subsequent dissolution of the Soviet Union under successor Boris

Yeltsin, Russia adopted the US model of a four-year presidential term with the possibility of only one reelection. Russian presidents, however, drink from the well of oriental illusions, and so Russian President Vladimir Putin sponsored a change in the country's Constitution by changing the four-year period to six-year. Russian presidents are now entitled to a term of six years with the possibility of reelection for another six years.

The most reckless backlash occurred in China. By the 1982 Constitution, which abolished the possibility of Maoist lifelongness, the President of the Republic began to have a five-year term, with the possibility of another subsequent period of the same duration. Since then the presidents have been serving ten years of power, always reelected once by Parliament. However, in 2018, shortly before being reelected for his second and last five-year term, President Xi Jinping sent to Parliament a proposal to abolish the limitation of terms. In theory, Chinese presidents may be reelected until the death. Since there is no prospect of parliamentary rebellion, especially under virtually lifelong state leadership, the interruption in life of a Chinese president's term will only occur by coup.

With the decision of Xi Jinping for the endless continuation of the presidential mandate, the great warlike danger of the world was once again around humanity. The major focus of warrior infection is no longer Berlin, Moscow, Sarajevo, Cairo or Tehran, but Beijing, most likely triggered by Piong-Yang, the capital of a country run by a fuze man, or, in the words of President Donald Trump, a rocket man.

Xi Jinping's policy appears even more arrogant when looking at developments in recent years. France, which in its Fifth Republic had been maintaining the status of a seven-year reelection for decades, adopted in the year 2000, during the presidency of Jacques Chirac, the five-year term. The president's right to reelection was maintained, but with five-year terms, just as in pre-Xi China. In Cuba, during the presidency of Raúl Castro, from 2008 to 2018, a five-year term was also instituted, with the right to only one reelection. In this, Cuba was following both France and China. With Xi Jinping's childlike example, great civilizational achievements are at serious risk.

Tripod. Is there reason to accept a lifetime chief of State?

It is clear at this point that one of the mainstays of the tripod of historical tragedy is the lifelongness of the chief of State. How should we see monarchy in this picture? Just like in the case of Republic with lifetime leadership. During the millennia in which humanity had the absolutist monarchy as a pattern of political organization, war was a constant.

After the end of World War II, Western Europe lived for over four decades without any war, until the outbreak of the Balkan War in Bosnia and Herzegovina, between 1992 and 2001. Among the reasons for this lasting peace were the work of the UN, fear of the use of atomic weapons, monetary stability, the strengthening of democracies, and the rejection of long-standing leaders in the most important countries, such as France, Italy and Germany, despite Franco's dictatorship in Spain. All European monarchies had already abandoned absolutism. In the so-called constitutional monarchies, the chief of State does not govern, only reigns. This means that, even having a mandate for life, the monarch does not interfere with the daily life of the subjects, which is a task of the prime minister. Whether taxes, school rules, the traffic code or labor laws change, it is all within the purview of the Parliament and the premier. The monarch, when aware of his position, does not even make public his opinion on any subject under discussion among legislators.

From the experience of many decades, humanity has some assurance that the constitutional monarchy, under the regime of the dictate "reigns but does not rule", poses little risk to peace.

There is no doubt, however, that the Republic, without long-lived chiefs, is safer. The only loss a country has in moving from monarchy to republic is the absence of a material or immaterial "public property janitor". This role in monarchies is exercised by the king or the emperor for life. It is a factor of emotional and cultural stability. But the cost, by the risk, is greater than the benefit. The Republic may, and shall, adopt the position of "public property janitor", who is not the President of the Republic, the Premier, the Supreme Court President, the Attorney General, or the Advocate General, but an official public with this specific function, which transcends periods of government. He preferably holds his office until his retirement. Since he should not get to the post at a young age, the time he has in office is not very long.

When the vandalism of ill-mannered people is no longer a problem for public administrations within a few decades or centuries, then the position of "public property janitor" may be extinguished.

In any case, it is the person of the chief of State, as mentioned above, who should not remain in the post for many years.

Our ancestors did not take from nowhere the idea of accepting a lifetime boss. This came from a misinterpretation of nature. Ants and bees, who have always been an example of hard work, have always had in their community a figure considered to be "queen". It was understood that she was the head of a "society". When we started forming human societies, instituting the position of "queen" for some strong person seemed very natural. What these humans discovered several millennia later was that there was no "queen" among the bees or among the ants. That big figure, served by thinner individuals, is nothing more than the mother of all those workers. A mother, no doubt, is for life.

A chief of State is far from being a mother. There is no reason for it to be long-lived, except for insisting on a childish misinterpretation.

The longevity of the chief, the first engine of the tragedy, is the letter **L** of Lifelongness. It is the first leg of the tragedy for a country.

Theocracy

The second leg is theocracy, letter **T**. For many centuries, lifelong monarchy and theocracy went together, for many monarchs were considered gods. Even after deity became something out of this world, as in the case of Aten, the sun god of Akhenaten, monarchs were the individuals who seemed to have direct contact with the Supreme Being. When Moses, leading the Jews through the wilderness for 40 years, entered the tent alone, or climbed alone on the mountain, it was understood that he was going to meet the deity. And when he said he had this contact, he was being honest, because that was what he felt. If he coined the tablets of the law, he did so in his intimacy, without witnesses, directly inspired by divinity. Who should doubt if he himself did not doubt?

Moses, as head of a people, was a theocrat, but that was the way to direct people at that time. His adoptive father, Pharaoh, was also a theocrat, as were almost all the chiefs of State at the time.

Were there wars all the time? Yes. Were the chiefs guilty of cultivating lifelongness and theocracy? Not even a little. They were far less guilty than doctors who in the eighteenth century applied bleeding as a method of healing and caused many patients to die early. These doctors relied on his method, and since every medical activity involves risk, the possibility of the patient's death was set on the table. If we can blame them a little for the deaths of patients, and none for the monarchs three millennia ago for the wars provoked, it is because these doctors received scientific training, with questioning and speculation.

But only with centuries of error and a great deal of imagination they could escape this crazy practice.

Theocracy presents an aggravation in relation to the mere lifelongness of the boss: thought is conditioned by dogmas. If there is an order to kill a woman because she is considered a witch, the receiver of the command does not hesitate. The order comes from a dogmatic certainty. One gives life without questioning, one takes life without questioning.

Christianity is a doctrine built on the content of a discourse, the Sermon on the Mount. In it, the most important point was the repeal of the Talion Law: If anyone hits you on one side, offer the other side. The recommendation not to respond evil to evil, violence to violence, aggression to aggression, is the basis of Christian doctrine regarding the behavior of the faithful.

The wars, however, did not cease. One reason was that while some were Christians, others were not, and to survive it was necessary to resist the enemy. The other, more decisive, reason was that governments were constituted as theocracies.

Leon Tolstoy, who learned Greek to read the Gospels in the original, developed the conviction that Christians did not practice true Christianity, by not following the central advice of the Sermon on the Mount. War, he said, makes no sense in Christian societies. Enlisting in the army is the greatest proof that one is not a Christian.

Tolstoy, however, paid no attention to a fundamental historical detail. At the Battle of Poitiers in 732, Charles Martel commanded the armies of France to defeat the Muslims, who had already dominated the Iberian Peninsula since the year 711, and now intended to advance by conquering France.

Charles Martel prevented the Arabs from entering, and as such they could not convert France, Germany, Poland and Russia as their purpose. Charles Martel received from the Catholic Church the title of "Hero of Christianity". Without him, there would almost certainly not have been the El Cid War of Reconquest, which began the expulsion of the Moors from Spain.

Without him, Tolstoy would almost certainly not be a Christian, but a Muslim. If Charles Martel had strictly followed the Sermon on the Mount, as Tolstoy thought every Christian should follow, he would have given up facing the Arabs. He would have accepted Muslim domination and Christianity would have disappeared from history, because the Italian Peninsula could not have resisted either.

How can one follow the recommendation not to respond to violence with violence? Now, this will happen when the causes of war are properly understood by the various armies and rulers of the world. The attitude of not wanting war has not been able to prevent it to this day. Therefore, it is not enough to reject. It is necessary to know why it occurs and why it presents itself before us as a categorical imperative.

It is not worth, for investigating the causes, to confuse them with any subterfuge. Matters of honor, questions of economic disputes, questions of ethnic differences are all grounds for propaganda, but none of these reasons is cause.

Recidivism. Did the return of theocracy in Persia inspire the Balkan War?

Even if at first glance the facts are unrelated, it is necessary to connect the points about the first war in Western Europe after the creation of the UN. These points are the following. In 1453, the Turkish-Ottoman Empire was finally able to enter Europe, taking advantage of the state of devastated earth resulting from the Hundred Years War, a conflict between France and England that actually lasted 116 years, from May 1337, to October 1453. Muslims carried their doctrine south of the Balkans and the Caucasus, but did not advance much further. Christian culture was very well established in the West, although religious practice did not show it. In any case, the first point of the fateful Balkan War was the Fall of Constantinople, taken by the Turks, in May 1453. France got rid of the British invasion, but at too high a cost. It should also be noted the resemblance to the end of World War I: There, at the end of the Middle Ages, the Fall of Constantinople awakened to a conclusion the struggling actors, who were France and England. In 1917, the fall of the Russian Empire played the same role in the spirits of the Western Allies, who now had England and France on the same side.

Let us now link to the other point. Christianity, as stated above, was consolidated, even without fuss and without great demonstrations of vigor, except for the Thirty Years' War of 1618-1648, of Protestants against Catholics, involving France, Germany, Spain, and the Italian Peninsula, among other powers. This conflict came as the final phase of the Dutch War of Independence against Spain, or the Eighty Years War, which lasted from 1568 to 1648. The war of Charles Martel in the eighth century continued and remains embedded in the popular imagination, constituting in an immense force to make Europeans resist the onslaught of any religions outside Christianity. To confront this consolidated Christian culture the 1979 Islamic Revolution arose in Persia, renamed Iran. This is another necessary point for understanding the reason of the Balkan War.

Bosnia. Which Balkan country has the highest Muslim proportion? Of the various Balkan states, the largest proportion of Muslims is Bosnia and Herzegovina. This was where the greatest dispute between the Roman Catholic Church and the Orthodox Catholic Church was concentrated, when, in the second half of the sixteenth century, the Turks arrived with their preaching in favor of Islam. It is understood today that they were most successful in that area because Christianity was not still very widespread there.

Around Serbia, at the end of World War II, the Republic of Yugoslavia was formed as a federation of six states: Serbia, Slovenia, Croatia, Bosnia and Herzegovina, Montenegro and Macedonia. Under Marshal Josip Broz Tito's command, it lasted officially from 1945 to 1992, when it was spun off, with each member State functioning as an independent Republic. At one point Tito launched the idea of adopting Spanish language teaching throughout the Union, as a means of obtaining a common instrument of communication between federative units. The idea did not prosper and when the marshal died, in 1980, leader Milosevic began to take measures that led to the dissolution of the bloc.

The Kosovo region had administrative autonomy within Serbia. Milosevic, in 1990, signed a measure that abolished this autonomy. In response, the Croatian Krajina region, which was populated by Serbs, declared independence, with Croatia and Slovenia also deciding to declare independence, followed by other units.

In Bosnia and Herzegovina, Muslims, with 49% of the population, form the dominant religion. The Orthodox Church has 35% and the Roman Catholic Church, only 13%, with Protestants having less than 1% of the inhabitants. In addition, the country, unlike others in the area, has no ethnic identity of its own, being formed by a population split in half by Serbs and Croats. With the declaration of independence of Slovenia and Croatia, Bosnia and Herzegovina's Serbian and Croatian pockets were treated as contested areas. When in January 1992, the European Community, now the European Union, recognized the independence of those two countries, the civil war took place among the

Bosnians.

With about half the population out of Christian culture, it was up to Bosnia and Herzegovina to break the long period of peace that Western Europe experienced after Hitler's death.

Afghanistan. Did expelling the Russians from Afghanistan bring anything better?

The Bosnian War officially ended in February 1994. At that time, a war developing in Afghanistan, the Russo-Afghan War (1978-1992), took new turns. On April 27, 1978, the People's Democratic Party seized power through a violent coup d'état, establishing a pro-Soviet government under the command of writer Nur Muhammad Taraki. In September 1979, Taraki was assassinated by order of then Prime Minister Hafizullah Amin, who came to rule as dictator. Inspired and inflated by the Islamic Revolution in Iran, young jihadist guerrillas, the mujahedines, had been attacking the government and perpetrating attacks for some months. The People's Democratic Party, after the overthrow of its leader Taraki, called for help from Moscow. Less than four months after Amin's coup, the Red Army intervened, beheading the dictator and imposing a new administration.

At that time, members of the Republican Party of the United States, especially Congressman Charlie Wilson, a Texas representative, had been campaigning to persuade wealthy businessmen to fund the mujahedin with weapons and money to expel the Russians from Afghanistan. The main motivation for this campaign was the assassination in February 1979 of the American ambassador in Kabul, Adolph Dubs. This led US conservatives to view the new administration of Afghanistan as an enemy of their interests there. The campaign was successful and the guerrillas were strengthened, to the surprise of the Soviet Army, which was under attack from all sides, having shot down aircraft and other equipment destroyed in explosions.

Nicknamed Soviet Vietnam, the Russo-Afghan War had the role of dismantling a powerful piece of internal propaganda, which for decades assured the inhabitants of the Soviet Union that the Stalinist administration would not wage external wars. Until then, the experience was to respond to invasions, such as those of the Nazi armies, or to promote swift interventions to reestablish allied governments, as had already happened in Prague. The setback in Afghanistan, when a mere change of government to strategically end a conflict period, resulted in a long war process. The Soviet government had no way of assessing in advance the weight of the youth's mood for the Islamic Revolution in Iran, even if it could guess the help that the US Republicans had been giving the rebels.

The Geneva Accords were signed in 1989, and they would lead to the Soviet withdrawal from the war, by Gorbachev's order, but the Afghan battles continued in practice until 1992, when the rule of the People's Democratic Party was overthrown by mujahedines.

On October 10, 1994, the organization called the Taliban was officially created, led by the mullah (priest) Mohammad Omar. The name comes from the Arabic word "Talib", which means "student". Put in the plural, the word in Afghanistan has come to mean "students of religion", or "seminarians". The current name of this group is "Islamic Emirate of Afghanistan", once the name "Taliban" lost its aura among young Muslims after the death of some of their influential leaders, especially Mullah Omar, in 2011.

Towns. How many thousands died in the fall of the WTC?

Although Iran's Islamic Revolution was the work of the Shiite sect, Islamists in other countries are almost all of the majority Sunni sect, which covers about 90 percent of Muslims. The word "Sunni" comes from "sunna", tradition, in Arabic. The term "Shiite" comes from "Shiat Ali", Ali's party, Ali being the son-in-law of the founder of Islam, Prophet Muhammad. Sunnis have their greatest strength in Saudi Arabia, while Shiites are more concentrated in Iran. These young jihadists in Afghanistan are Sunni, and have received membership from many Sunnis in other countries, particularly Saudi Arabia.

One of those "students" migrating to Afghanistan was Osama Bin Laden, a young Saudi from a wealthy industrial family.

While conservative sectors of the US Republican Party have helped the Taleban, including Osama Bin Laden's group, in struggling against the Russians with money, weapons and methods, the likelihood of winning the heart of Islamic youth in the Middle East and the Near East to the American cultural cause was tiny. Just as the alliance with Stalin against Hitler would not result in peaceful coexistence between the US government and the former seminarian of the Kremlin, so would the Taleban receive US assistance beared in the Emperor Vespasian's saying, "pecunia non olet" (money doesn't stink).

It was in this spirit that in August 1988 Osama Bin Laden created the al Qaeda (The Base) group, a campaign movement for the expansion of Islam at all costs, including violent actions. Unlike what the Taliban had been doing so far in Afghanistan, which has focused more on its region, al Qaeda has become a world-wide entity. Money for that was not lacking in Bin Laden's hands.

Small suicide bombings or car bomb explosions in supermarkets would not give al Qaeda the projection it wanted to have. In this way, an action was planned in the United States.

Thirteen years after the group's operations began, the boldest terrorist act in history was unleashed against New York City on September 11, 2001.

Young suicides, a kind of 21st century kamikaze, were instructed in flight simulators to act as pilots. If they had undergone regular training in airplanes themselves, there would have been the possibility of being discovered. Experienced airmen who have analyzed the type of flight these young men have made, undoubtedly concluded that they were laboratory pilots, that is, they learned to handle aircraft using only computers, not airplanes. When they held the rudder of the vehicle, it was finally only for the fatal flight.

At other times, at the time, for example, of the first version of the movie "King Kong," the symbolic building of New York was the 381-meter-high Empire State. But in 1973, the 417-meter-high Twin Towers complex building (541-meter-high adding the antenna) was inaugurated, in the place where the *World Trade Center* became operational. The two towers, hitherto the tallest buildings in the world, lasted until 2001, because they collapsed under the attack of two planes on them on that fateful morning of September 11th, also called 11S.

The planes hijacked by the terrorists were four, and this was the number of buildings they intended to bring down. A group of 19 jihadists split into four kidnappings, two of them diverted to the Twin Towers. A third plane hit and shot down a wing of the Pentagon, the headquarters of the United States Department of Defense in Virginia. The fourth plane was intended to hit the Capitol, seat of Congress, according to information obtained from passengers. These, bearing the news of the attack on the Twin Towers, advanced on the pilot and the other terrorists in the cabin as they flew over Shanksville, Pennsylvania. As they were about to die, they preferred to save the lives of parliamentarians and House and Senate officials. The plane crashed right there in Pennsylvania.

The four hijacked and damaged planes were regular commercial flight aircraft and were in service, all packed with passengers.

The bombings that morning resulted in 3,016 deaths, a few dozen missing and more than 5,000 injured.

The immediate consequence of these acts was a change in the control of passenger entry on commercial flights, which was now much stricter. The influx of immigrants into the country also suffered a shock, especially about people from Islamic countries. Then-President of the United States, George Walker Bush, announced the policy of the "War on Terrorism", or "War on Terror".

Terrorism. What was inspired by the group "Popular Will"?

In the modern world, the terrorism of individuals against the State arose among Russian revolutionaries fighting the monarchy in the late nineteenth century. Vladimir Lenin's older brother Aleksander Ulianov, a young zoologist awarded for his scientific work, joined the guerrilla group "People's Will" and launched an attack on the life of Tsar Alexander III. He was hanged on May 20th, 1887, at the age of 21. This execution impressed on the spirit of Lenin, a son of educated middle-class civil servants, the purpose of fighting with all means against the imperial power. Personal experience led him later to develop a peculiar concept of "imperialism": this would not only be the power of kings, but the power exercised by the big capital in rich and powerful countries, resulting in the exploitation of poor countries. The identification of "big capital" with "imperialism" was convenient for revolutionary propaganda, but it represented a shift in the theoretical basis of the philosophers of "scientific socialism", once it embodied the intention to "skip" the historical phase of the market economy. It also resumed the analysis of David Ricardo's "theory of comparative advantages", but with inverted sign in relation to the understanding of the English economist. Asked about the plan for the abolition of the State, he replied that the State to be abolished was the "bourgeois State", and this had already happened through the Russian Revolution. Dream of some and nightmare of others, this abolition never really happened.

The Russian activists of the People's Will were inspired by the "Kingdom of Terror", a classification given by the Girondins to the Jacobin period led by Robespierre in the French Revolution. According to the Girondins and the royalists, Robespierre had installed the "State terrorism". In ancient Greece, philosophers defended the legitimacy of tyrannicide, with arguments justifying the right of any ordinary citizen to murder the ruler who became an unbearable tyrant. The idea was shelved during the Christian antiquity and the High Middle Ages, until St. Thomas Aquinas, rescuing to scholasticism the texts of Aristotle and others, spoke about the right to rebellion. It was in the French Revolution, denying the transcendentalist religion, that the rebels applied the right to rebellion, first beheading authorities, politics and scientists, then doing the same to citizens who disagreed with State policy. These events resurfaced in Russia a century later.

The triumph of the Russian Revolution at the end of 1917 inspired terrorist groups in various regions of the world, not only in proletarian struggles, but also in the host of the shabby-proletariat, factions that would support Nazi-fascism. Among these groups was one that attacked the English administration on Palestinian territory, taken from Turkey at the end of World War I, in 1917. In the division of the Ottoman Empire's booty spread across the Maghreb, the Near East, and the Middle East, it fell to Great Britain the possession of Palestinian territory, where the city of Jerusalem was located. The Israelites, who had been intensifying reoccupation of the area since the late nineteenth century, and even more since the onset of World War, called for the restoration of the State of Israel. The *Irgun* (Organization, in Hebrew), or Irgun Zvai Leumi, founded in 1931, was one among those groups, and it was constituted as a paramilitary force. In one of his bomb attacks, he destroyed the British administration building. In 1940, he became a political party, the *Herut Party* (Freedom Party) with wide popular acceptance, with one of the leaders having the future Nobel Peace Prize Menachem Begin. In the wake of Israel's independence boom in 1948, Albert Einstein, Hannah Arendt, and several other Jewish family intellectuals published a letter in the New York Times warning Israelis against Herut, whose methods and principles they compared with those of the fascist and Nazi parties of Europe. In 1973 Herut merged with other smaller parties forming the *Likud* (Consolidation).

Many twentieth-century guerrilla groups were strengthened by the echoes of Lenin's preaching that great capital and imperialism are one only thing, and it is up to the proletariat to confront and defeat it to escape oppression. Terrorist acts were an ominous consequence of adhering to this doctrine.

German researchers profiled terrorist minds by interviewing and analyzing detainees. For most of these individuals, there is a common trajectory: social oppression in the early days, going underground later, and finally developing a friend-foe sense of dichotomy in the consolidation of a fanatical Manichaeism.

There are media companies that recommend avoiding the words "terrorism" and "terrorist", given the diffuse meaning they have taken, both in terms of actions and purposes. In fact, treating a fanatical young man who is willing to act in extreme violence with adjectives such as "terrorist" or "radical" can act as an incentive to his action. Not only do they want to be treated as terrorists or radicals, but they also want, even if they die in the attacks, to leave their name in the mainstream press.

The plans for the attack on the Twin Towers involved turning the tragedy into a great pyrotechnic spectacle, even at the early hours of the morning, so that the news would reverberate throughout the day. Since that jihad ("effort") involved 19 suicide commanders, their names did not matter, but the name of the person of the operation's architect and financier, Osama Bin Laden.

The press would have many adjectives to choose from, so as not to lend any glamor to terrorists. Lunatics (as Bertrand Russell proposed to call the Nazis), fanatics, extremists, and rebels are some of these terms.

Taliban. How long did the Taliban dictatorship last in Afghanistan?

In April 1992 the leading Islamic factions fighting in Afghanistan signed the Peshawar Agreement (Pehawar, Pakistan), which would guide the administration after the fall of the People's Democratic Party. As chief of State was recognized the name of the old mujahedin leader Sibghatullah Mojaddedi. In late May the factions agreed to swear in Hekmatyar as prime minister. A week later, he murdered the chief of State to take his post. A new phase of fighting began in what became known as the *Afghan Civil War*. The capital was almost completely destroyed and more than 50,000 civilians were killed over the next two years.

In August 1994, with support from Pakistan, Mullah Mohammad Omar led an action that murdered the leading "warlords", marched to Kandahar and took over the city. The Taliban, headed by Omar, seized power and installed their Islamic dictatorship. In their tenure, the Taliban destroyed Buddha statues recognized as a World Heritage Site by UNESCO, forced women into burqa, instituted systematic stoning of women accused of adultery, and enlisted boys in the army. These, according to allegations that appeared later, suffered abuse by the adult soldiers.

This grotesque Taliban dictatorship lasted seven years. It would have lasted much longer, under the watchful eye of the powers to the east and west, who no longer intended to intrude on that swampy terrain if the attacks on the Twin Towers in September 2001 had not been quickly clarified as Taliban action, specifically those of the Taliban led by Osama bin Laden.

On October 7th, England and the United States launched air strikes on the cities of Kabul, Herat and Kandahar. With these and other offensives, the rebel Islamic group called the Northern Alliance advanced to the capital and, on November 9th, displaced the mujahedin occupying it, ending the Taliban government In December the *Bonn Agreement* was signed in Europe, setting the terms for the Afghan government through the International Security Assistance Force. On the 21st the provisional government resulting from the agreement was installed.

The overthrow of the Taliban, however, did not bring peace. Fighting continued in both Afghanistan and the border areas of Pakistan. Amid Karzai emerged as leader, occupying the presidency of the Republic. On October 9th, 2004, there were direct presidential elections, which were won by Amir Karzai. On December 7th he was officially inaugurated.

Iraq. Why did Saddam Hussein become a religious man?

As the Afghan war continued, President George W. Bush, the Pentagon, and other major US officials realized, shortly after the Taliban overthrow, that the "War on Terror" would not succeed if actions were restricted to Afghanistan.

Iraq, ruled by dictator Saddam Hussein since 1979, was seen as a second focus of jihadist generation. In addition, there were precedents of friction between the Iraqi government and the United States government. Despite US support for the Iran-Iraq war in the early 1980s, a halo of distrust arose, over allegations that Saddam Hussein used chemical weapons to promote genocide among Kurdish Iraqis, mostly Christians. .

The final straw for the beginning of hostilities with Saddam Hussein came on August 2nd, 1990, when Iraq invaded Kuwait, the British-allied constitutional monarchy in the far south of Iraq. Saddam had accused little Kuwait of sucking Iraqi oil wells, sharing the same shafts, and sabotaging OPEC (Organization of the Petroleum Exporting Countries) by selling oil cheaper than neighboring countries.

President George Herbert Bush, who ruled the United States in the early 1990s, formed a coalition with the English, French and other allies, and declared war on Iraq, in early 1991, to force Saddam Hussein to withdraw his troops from Kuwait. This war, led by the three allies of

World War I and World War II, would have been World War III if other countries had lined up next to Iraq. This did not happen, and soon Saddam Hussein left Kuwait, not without causing great damage to the neighboring country, setting the main oil wells on fire in the region.

With no connection to the great Sunni, Shiite, and Christian religions of Iraq, although he came from a Sunni family, Saddam Hussein had always been agnostic. Under close Allied fire, his behavior changed. He came to declare himself an Islamic loyalist and to appeal for the unity of the Muslim peoples against Christians in Europe and America.

The desire to stay in power for life worked the "miracle" of turning an anti-religious man into a fervent follower of the Quran.

The withdrawal of Iraqi troops from Kuwait was not enough to make Saddam Hussein reliable in the eyes of the leaders of the great powers. The UN Security Council imposed several sanctions on the country, including air blocking, and sent inspector teams to try to locate chemical weapons depots. There is, however, an important detail to this surveillance work: it began only after a period of about two years after the Allied attacks. This represented sufficient time for the transfer of stockpiles to safe places, for example in some large underground compartment.

UN agents were unable to locate chemical weapons, even with the certainty that this prohibited type of ammunition was used against Kurdish populations.

On March 20th, 2013, the invasion of Iraq began, with soil, naval and air troops. Under the leadership of US President George Walker Bush, son of George Herbert Bush, a coalition of countries was formed including Britain, Spain, Australia, Poland, Portugal and others. France, which participated in the bombings in 1991, decided this time to stay out of the alliance.

The goals, according to George Walker Bush, were first to locate weapons of mass destruction, once Saddam Hussein "did not collaborate with UN inspectors", and, secondly, to locate potential terrorists. The by-product would obviously be the overthrow of Saddam Hussein, who was not an explicit target, since it is clear from the Pentagon doctrine that the United States cannot directly attack any foreign chief of State.

With the invasion and successful escape of Saddam Hussein through the defense tunnels patiently built years earlier in Iraq's capital Baghdad, the United States seized the administration of the country until

April 2005, when President Jalal Talabani was elected and sworn in. Under the American administration, numerous suicide bombings and car bombs followed. One of them, on August 19, 2003, hit the UN diplomatic building, headed by Sergio Vieira de Mello, who was killed along with many officials.

On December 13th, 2003, Saddam Hussein was located in a tunnel in the north of the country by men from the Kurdistan regional army and the United States Army.

In November 2006, the former dictator was tried and sentenced to death, along with two other collaborators. The then President Jalal Talabani, who was Catholic and did not accept to sign the death sentence issued by the Iraqi Criminal Court. He resigned from office for a few weeks, and then his legal substitute signed the document. The former dictator, shortly before being taken to the gallows, cursed the judges and the interveners, who thwarted his lifelong mandate.

As for mass destruction weapons, which was not found at the time of the invasion, and had been one of the two reasons for the intervention, according to the New York Times they did not exist at all and the US president was lying when he said he would find them. Following the expiration of George W. Bush's term, under Barack Obama, investigators found such weapons in Iraq. The New York Times published the news almost imperceptibly. Most US and world citizens continued to think that these weapons were never found.

Neo-caliphate. What young forces initially joined the Islamic State?

The merchant Muhammed, or Muhammad, founder of the Muslim religion, was, in the most legitimate theocratic tradition, a mixture of priest, general and politician. In Islam, he is recognized as the last prophet, whose predecessors are Abraham, Moses, and Jesus. Obviously, to make the presence of a new prophet more credible in a more Catholic than Jewish area, as the Middle East of the Arabian Peninsula and Mesopotamia was in the seventh century, it was necessary to alter the role and history of Jesus of Nazareth. For Islam, Jesus did not resuscitated, for Allah deceived the authorities of the Sanhedrin, causing Judas Iscariot to carry the cross at one point of the Via Crucis and leading Jesus to flee through the crowd. Judas was crucified and killed in the place of Jesus of Nazareth.

When Muhammed died in Medina in July 632, there was a phase of rebellion in his empire over power struggles. In the same year leader

Abu Bakr managed to defuse the hotbeds of resistance and established himself as caliph. A caliph is the supreme head of a country that adopts Islam as a State religion. This State is now understood as a caliphate.

After Abu Bakr, the first caliph, three more caliphs followed in Medina. These four form the period of the Orthodox Caliphate, when chiefs were elected by the Muslim community.

In the year 661, it was established the Damascus-based Umayyad Caliphate, already under the Sunni orientation, which recognizes only hereditary caliphs, of Muhammed's lineage.

In 756 the caliphate's headquarters moved from Damascus to Kufa, and six years later it settled in the new city of Baghdad, operating there until 1258. Só the Abbasid Caliphate phase began. More than a century later, with the reign of the fifth Abbasid caliph, Harun al-Rashid (Aaron the Just), and with the city of Baghdad already consolidated as capital, what is known as the "Golden Age" of Islam took place. Al-Rashid founded in his city the House of Wisdom, as a successor institution of the Academy of Athens and the Museum of Alexandria. It was there that al-Khwarizmi developed Algebra, for example. From 711 to 1249, Islam dominated the Iberian Peninsula, creating there the Province of Andalusia. In 1258, already without the western provinces of the Iberian Peninsula and Maghreb (North Africa), and also by the rise of the Turkish army, the so-called Mamluk, Baghdad fell under the invasion of the army of Hulagu Khan, nephew of Genghis Khan.

Still in 1258, the Abbasid Caliphate settled in Cairo, operating there until the 16th century.

In 1517 the Ottoman Caliphate began in the city of Constantinople, renamed Istanbul. With the defeat in World War I, the Ottoman Empire was dissolved and the Constitution of 1924 abolished the position of caliph. The last caliph, however, Abdul Mejid II, was vested in the post in 1926, by Islamic religious. He died in Paris in 1944. It was the 101st caliph in all history.

In 2014, 70 years after the death of the last caliph, a fanatical group emerged in Iraq as a result of the policy of Allied intervention, establishing in the city of Mosul the seat of a so-called caliphate. It was the so-called Islamic State of Iraq and the Levant, a clandestine State that dominated vast areas of eastern Syria and northern Iraq. Its leader, Ibrahim Awwad Ibrahim Ali al-Badri al-Samarrai, adopted the pseudonym Abu Bakr al-Baghdadi to honor the first caliph.

This Ibrahim al-Samarrai is not a school dropout. Quite the contrary, he studied master and doctorate. Not in Classical Letters or

Engineering. His diplomas are in Islamic Theology. No reading of Dostoevsky, Buddhist texts, Thomas Aquinas or Spinoza. If one has deeply studied a given subject and the contradictory point in this trajectory has been missing, then the most important element has been missing: Thought.

The participation of the interveners in the formation of their group certainly occurred indirectly. Paul Bremer, the civilian administrator who the United States has appointed to run Iraq in the name of the coalition that toppled Saddam Hussein's regime, has instituted a $ 10 daily allowance for young Iraqi workers across the country. For those living conditions, it was a good salary.

When President Jalal Talabani was elected and the coalition gradually shifted decision-making to local authorities, that allowance was cut. The new government of the country did not put anything in place and those young people began to face great financial difficulties. A few oil tycoon sheiks began to fund opposition groups. One of these groups, which grew the most, was exactly that of Ibrahim al-Samarrai.

While feeling abandoned by the new government, those young people who contributed to the occupation and were paid for it largely adhered to the calls of the Islamic State group.

Bondage. What fraction of the Kurdish people were enslaved by the Islamic State?

Enslavement of young women to serve as the sexual object of the militants became a common practice among the fanatics of that group. They mainly captured Kurdish teenagers of the Yazidi religion on the grounds that the Yazidi are followers of Satan and must be led astray from their creed, and slavery is justified until conversion occurs.

According to Yazidi theology, the Creator first produced seven angels, or "seven mysteries," as emanations of his own spirit, and gave them orders to obey Him always. When Adam was created, made of dust, the Creator commanded the seven angels to bow to him. Six angels obeyed, but not *Melek Taus* (Peacock Angel), saying it made no sense to bow to Adam, made of dust, while he, an angel, was part of the very spirit of divinity. In recognition of his bravery and intelligence, the Creator appointed him chief of the other angels and ruler of the universe. Once everything that happens to be good or bad in the world depends on him, he was punished for errors that occurred on Earth. Thrown into the pit of fire, he repented, and his tears put out the fire. Then he returned to his command post.

Under Islamic theology, the fallen angel, *Shaitan* (Satan), also refused to bow to Adam, but this was interpreted as a show of arrogance and pride, weighing on the condemnation, which was never reversed. Because of this coincidence over their reverence for Adam, Islamists understand that the Yazidi worship Satan, by identifying the Peacock Angel with the devil. Whith regard to Catholicism, a majority religion among the Kurds, the Yazidis also have a point of conflict, once they believe in reincarnation, like first-century Gnostic Christians and 13th century Cathars did. Catholics, however, do not identify them with devil worshipers.

Just as Hitler used radio to spread his fanaticism, Ibrahim al-Samarrai made intensive use of the internet. Through this vehicle he attracted faithful young people from Islam, whether of family tradition or recent converts, not only from Iraq and Syria, but also from Europe, America and other parts of the world. The many videos on the world wide web showing decapitations of "infidels", far from scaring the young supporter of the cause, served to engage him even more. Among the cases of beheadings scattered through video recordings were that of a reporter who came from Japan to report on the group's performance and that of a row of Coptic Catholics on mission in Libya.

Not only people going into the territory that Ibrahim al-Samarrai was dominating were in danger of dying. Attacks perpetrated in various parts of the world were attributed to the fanatic group. One of the most shocking was the shooting of 12 journalists from the satirical magazine Charlie Hebdo in Paris on January 7th, 2015. Several other actions, from lone wolves or small fanatical groups, took place in France again, Spain, Switzerland, Indonesia, Russia, and many other countries.

Aware that Iraq and Syria could not defeat the group alone, the United States convened a meeting with representatives from seven other countries (Germany, Australia, Canada, France, Italy, the United Kingdom, and Turkey) to form a fighting coalition. against the Islamic State group. The summoned ministers took the proposal to their governments and the proposal was accepted. Already in 2014, the fanatics began to suffer heavy bombing. Ahead, three dozen other countries joined the offensive. Iraqi Prime Minister Professor Haider al-Abadi was able to retake Mosul in July 2017. Since then, the fate of the Islamic State group has turned sour. From that time until the beginning of 2019, all territories were rescued for the governments of Iraq and Syria, even though Syria's lifetime government is facing civil war with several other militias scattered throughout the country since 2011.

Ibrahim al-Samarrai, the self-proclaimed caliph of the Islamic State, which the Coalition thought had died under bombardment among the thousands dumped on the fanatical bases, resurfaced in the middle of the first half of 2019, claiming participation as a remote commander in the attacks on Sri Lanka a few weeks earlier. On October 29, 2019, however, President Donald Trump announced that, located and surprised by United States military personnel, al-Samarrai, or al-Baghdadi, had fled through a tunnel, accompanied by his three minor children. When he saw that the tunnel had no way out, he fired bombs on his body, dying along with the three children.

Even without territory under their rule, and finally without the presence of the founding chief, analysts have noted that the gang still has strong firepower. Only time will tell whether the death of the founding leader will empty the group or not.

Groups

In addition to the People's Will, the Irgun, the Taliban, the al Qaeda and the Islamic State group, many other extremist organizations have become famous for terrorist acts.

Klan. The Ku Klux Klan group was formed in the United States in December 1865, by slave-like individuals revolted by their defeat in the Civil War. It continued to kill black people until the early decades of the twentieth century.

RAFC. The Revolutionary Armed Forces of Colombia form a group that emerged in 1964 and served in the jungles for 54 years, intending to implant the dictatorship of the proletariat in Colombia, until being transformed into a political party by peace agreement in 2017.

Sendero. The Communist Party of Peru Sendero Luminoso (PCP-SL, SL: Shining Path) initiated terrorist actions in 1980 with the aim of establishing a peasant proletarian dictatorship, inspired in Mao Zedong. In 1992 its top leader, Abimael Guzman Reynoso was arrested, which weakened the group.

ETA The Euskadi Ta Askatasuna (ETA - Basque Homeland and Freedom) was a clandestine army fighting for independence in the Basque region of northern Spain, having committed numerous attacks throughout its existence. This and other groups that intended to make their provinces independent countries in Europe lost their sense of existence with the Treaty of Lisbon, which in December 2007 determined the creation of the presidency of the European Union;

Jihad. Egyptian Islamic Jihad began its activities in the 1970s. It was behind the assassination of President Anwar al-Sadat in 1981. It is currently an arm of al Qaeda.

Boko-Haram. The fanatical group Boko Haram ("Non-Islamic Education is a Sin") has been operating in Nigeria since 2002, perpetrating attacks and abducting teenage girls to indoctrinate them on their principles.

Al-Shabbaab. Harakat a-Shabbaab al-Mujahedin, or just al-Shabbaab ("The Youth" in Arabic), is a Somali-based fanatical organization linked to al Qaeda. It even prevented for ten years the installation of any government in the country. UN Peacekeepers were systematically murdered, identified by their ethnic characteristics. Finally, the African Union Army, whose soldiers could be mistaken for Somali people, disrupted the bandit groups that smothered and vandalized administrative bodies, universities, hospitals and other institutions. In the year 2000, finally, the country managed to form the Transitional Federal Government.

Several dozen other groups fanatized by religious creeds - through the representatives of the prophets -, or by secular creeds - through the atheistic "messiahs" proclaimed "genius guides" -, are still spreading around the world, committing violent actions until measures are taken that make their existence obsolete, as the European Union has done with ETA, the Irish Republican Arm (IRA) and others.

(🖐) If one decides to trade politically, or diplomatically, with a fanatic, one should prepare to lose. To the fanatic, the possibility of negotiation involving ideas is completely forbidden. The ability to present a second option, plan B, is a waste of time. To the fanatic, everything is based on "all or nothing", "black and white", "without concession". But if there is gain or loss for him, this is not by negotiation, because in his monolithic view the path and destiny are already determined, with no chance of change.

The third leg that makes up the tripod of the tragedy is the installation of new capital, as long as it houses the chief of State.

Capitalnovism

Some countries built cities to work as administrative capitals, setting up the prime minister and his deputies. If the chief of State was kept in the traditional capital, city with secular historical capital status, then little or no disturbance was observed in the economic and cultural fields.

Serious problems occurred when some willful leader decided to set up the chief of State's residence in a city without this historical status, whether it was a newly built agglomeration or a settlement that had been in existence for decades or centuries.

Some books already published by this author, such as *The Brussels Crisis*, deal with the subject, but it does not cost to explain it again.

Historical observations show that the time required to consolidate a new capital that houses the chief of State is between 120 and 130 years. In that same period, a city that once had historical status loses it, if it is oblivious of the commander in chief's presence.

History and Geography books prior to the 21st century treat the capitals of countries as a neutral administrative phenomenon, because Social Psychology was not part of the theoretical framework of these works - the term "capitalnovism" would not have made sense there. Therefore, it is appropriate to study them to know where the French king Louis XVI resided in the years before the French Revolution, but not to know that the city of Versailles, housing the monarch, could be the cause of some social turmoil. In fact, the correlations are there, recorded, but not the cause and effect relationships. If some ancient author established this link, he was then placing the cart before the horse.

New. Is a leader who leaves consolidated capital a New Man?

Capitalnovism (letter **C**) is not a psychic deviation that affects a well-formed chief of State prepared behind the scenes of current politics. Capitalnovism is a thing of person who in Old Rome was called a "new man". Certainly the commander in chief, if weak in personality, can be led to make the decision, convinced by some aide who is a victim of the disease. This may have been the case with Louis XIV, who built the Palace of Versailles as a summerhouse, but eventually established the court and government there in 1682.

A plausible hypothesis is that Louis XIV yielded to appeals from his secretary of State (prime minister), Jean-Baptiste Colbert. This had been private secretary of Cardinal Mazarin, his predecessor in the leadership of government. Endowed with unmatched competence, when the cardinal was about to die, he recommended him to the king, asking him to take advantage of his services. He created the Academy of Sciences (1666), the Paris Observatory (1667) and the Royal Academy of

Architecture (1671). As a ruler, he cleaned up the State finances. He did not live to see the collapse of his work in later decades, for he died in 1683, the year after the court was installed in Versailles. From within the Champagne region, it was reported that his family was descended from Scottish nobles, but no one was able to prove it. A strong indication that Colbert was a "new man" was his nepotism, which employed numerous family members in the public sector. Napoleon later did something similar, swearing in his close relatives as emperors of neighboring countries, but he was not mad to remove the French administration from Paris and return to Versailles, where Louis XVI was torn off by the March of Women on October 6, 1789.

The same phenomenon of auxiliary action may have occurred in antiquity when Alexander the Great decided to build Alexandria, the new capital of his kingdom on the coast of Egypt. Son of Philip II of Macedonia and educated by Aristotle and Menaechmus, it is almost certain that he was convinced of the desirability of creating the capital from the ideas of one of his three trusted generals. Plutarch, his biographer, says the idea came up in a dream, in which an elder recited a verse from Homer who speaks of the Isle of Faros on the coast of Egypt. That this dream should become a capital must have received the finger of one of his strategists. Another hypothesis is that Alexander may not have been a natural son of Philip, who came to reject his wife Olympias of Epirus on the grounds that he had seen her sleeping with a snake. The fact is that Olympias returned to her hometown of Dodona, but her uncle Arribas, seeing that she was pregnant, convinced her to return to Philip.

Constantine, who ascended the throne for his ability as a general, did not need an auxiliary to assist him in moving the capital. As a "new man", he left Rome and established the seat of the kingdom in Byzantium, calling it Constantinople, the Rome of the East, today the Turkish city, called Istanbul.

The tripod of the historical tragedy, the ethological generator of wars between peoples, is complete, acting at times with its three legs, but also with two or only one. There are three decisions, three ways of life and three misfortunes, born of human weakness, either by the arts of mere ignorance or by megalomania. These legs are: 1) Lifelongness (**L**); 2) Theocracy (**T**); 3) Capitalnovism (**C**).

Costs

The reader may be thinking of new capitals that worked. The reader will be mistaken, however, if imagines that they consolidated without the cost of much blood.

Let us consider three notable cases: Madrid, Washington-DC and Tokyo.

Madrid. Was there a price revolution in Spain before Madrid?

In 1556 Philip II became king of Spain, Sicily and Sardinia, becoming also, in the phase of the union of the Iberian crowns, king of Portugal and Algarves, what added Brazil to all the rest of Latin America, which already was Hispanic He was also king of the Netherlands. In the fifth year of his reign, 1561, he was dedicated to installing the capital in a central city of the Spanish plateau, having chosen Madrid.

In 1568, Jean Bodin pioneered theorizing about the Price Revolution, a process that had been going on for decades, but reached stunning levels under Philip II. By the hypothesis of Jean Bodin, prices were upwardly driven by the inflow of precious metals brought from Latin America to Europe, especially silver from Potosi mines, in present-day Bolivia. He had no better explanation in the sixteenth century. The fact is that the most assured disaster of the establishment of the chief of State in capital without secular historical status is the pathological pressure to raise prices in what the twentieth century characterized as an inflationary impulse. As a result of this economic breakdown, Spain lost control on Netherlands, which won its independence, and also saw the Invincible Armada sunk in the English Channel, defeated by the English.

Even before the Industrial Revolution brought the power of the British to the brink of glory, they had been dominating the seas, taking the place of the Iberians, who in the sixteenth century had conquered the four corners of the world. The attitude of Philip II, transferring the royal residence from Granada to Madrid, promoted, without the British to this day recognizing the cause, the change, from Romanesque Europe to the Anglo-Saxon world, of hegemonic power over the whole Earth. Portugal had dominated almost all of South America, various regions of Africa, much of India, parts of China and islands of Indonesia, and had explored all of Australia without having contingents to colonize it. Spain dominated southern and western South America, all of Central America,

Mexico, and nearly all of the present-day United States, the Philippines, and regions of Africa. The world was Iberian until the defeat of the Invincible Armada in 1588. Madrid consolidated itself as a capital, but lost world prominence.

Washington DC. How did the United States protect its currency?

In the year 1800 the United States leaders, separated from the British crown since 1776, left the capital Philadelphia and installed the presidential residence in the new capital Washington-DC (DC: *District of Columbia*). In the Anglo-American War, of 1812, the English burned down and destroyed the capital, but it was later rebuilt with more architectural care and greater commitment.

As the French economic disaster that led to the Revolution was much alive in the memory of the various countries, the US-Americans tried to protect their currency, what was done with the establishment of the gold standard by Alexander Hamilton, in 1789, in his first year as treasury secretary, a new position created by President George Washington. The gold standard was not a very new idea. It was theoretically launched by David Hume in London in 1752, but in that year of the French Revolution it was an obvious practical necessity. With it, of course, inflation is avoided, but not the other problems emanating from the new capital, such as dearness itself.

All breakdown proceeds from the social practice of disregard for established symbols. Without currency protection, it will be the first institution to suffer from fever, a fever that is automatically quantified, and that leaves the economy shaken. Under efficient protection, as was the gold standard, that fever is controlled, but not the other tissue disruptions that generate that symptom. The Anglo-American War was just one of many war eruptions on US territory in the 19th century, and the British attempt to retake the colony was certainly encouraged by the problems the crown saw in the administration of the former colony. Wars with Mexico, which turned this huge country into a small-land country, were ultimately a gain because the fighting was stronger in the Americans, but they probably would not have happened without the destructiveness produced by the new capital.

Many wars with the indigenous people also erupted, much more often than in other areas of the New World, especially compared to Canada, where these wars did not exist. All of this was happening until the greatest conflict in the Americas was present with all its overwhelming momentum, which was the American Civil War, or

Secession Crisis, from 1861 to 1865.

Before the 21st century, the motivations of the wars were identified, not the causes, so that this immense conflict, the American Civil War, was explained as having been motivated by the difference in economic conception between a group, poor and agrarian, of southern States, and the majority part of the territory, formed by the north, richer and more industrialized. The southern governors of the so-called Confederate States did not accept the abolition of slavery, a growing demand from the north.

As we now know, the cause lies in the tripod of the historical tragedy, using at least one of the three legs. The United States was free of theocracy and was moving to rid itself of governmental lifelongness, so the root cause of the American Civil War was the Ravenna Effect, or capitalnovism, the social pathology caused by the establishment of the residence of the chief of State. in a city without a secular historical capital status.

The Southern Confederates, who represented the rebel side of the new nationality, rejected the capital Washington-DC, by setting up their headquarters, their provisional government, in Richmond, Virginia. The conflict was therefore a war between the recent capital of the United States, still far from being consolidated, and the attempt to break with the installation of another new capital by opponents of the end of the slave regime.

Finally, after more than 800,000 deaths on both sides, General Ulysses S. Grant's forces seized Richmond on April 1st, 1865, with a troop made up almost exclusively of black soldiers. It was the XXV Union Corps. On the 3rd, General Robert E. Lee led his Confederate army west, but suffered a further defeat at *Sayler's Creek*, realizing that he had no chance. On the 9th he signed the act of surrender in the *Appomattox Court House*, Southern Virginia.

The two most notable negative consequences of the war were the assassination of President Abraham Lincoln, on April 15th, and the formation of the Ku Klux Klan, which for decades promoted murders of black people in revenge for the victory of the abolitionists in 1865.

President Lincoln had promised that after the eventual victory of the Union, he would immediately enforce the act of abolition of slavery signed in 1863, which indeed happened. His murder is regarded as the first great revenge of the defeated.

The positive side of the postwar era was the policy taken as a point of honor by the Union government to develop the southern states and use all resources to stop US federative units from showing economic and social significant differences between each other.

A few years before the Secession Crisis, another major war took place in North America, which was the Mexico-United States War, or the Mexican-American War, from 1846 to 1848. This conflict, also provoked by capitalnovism, resulted in the incorporation, by the United States, of large extent of the western lands, formerly belonging to Mexico. This one lost 50% of its territory.

As for the consolidation of the capital, this fact occurred only after the Great Depression, of 1929.

Tokyo. Did the new capital Tokyo provoke the Japanese diaspora?

Emperor Mutsuhito, whose posthumous name is Meiji Tenno and is therefore called in Japan Emperor Meiji, and also the initiator of the current Meiji dynasty, came to power in 1867, at the age of 14. In accord with samurai and daimyo, he ended, as a result of the Boshin War, the era of the Tokugawa shogunate, which split the country into more than 250 autonomous regions. In 1869 he moved the capital from Kyoto to Tokyo, initiating a series of major transformations, such as the installation of the Senate (1875) and the National Assembly (1890). Understanding this political modernization as part of Japan's insertion in the practices of the modern world, the most important and exemplary positive measure taken by him was the education reform in 1872, with the intended and achieved goal of providing free public education at the basic level for all Japanese children. His appreciation for reading and writing is proven in his poetic production, once he has authored over 10,000 tankas, always using perfect metric.

Just as the United States under the Ravenna Effect provoked by Washington-DC incorporated large territories formerly belonging to its neighbor Mexico, Japan began heavy wars with its neighbors, one of its achievements abroad being Korea's annexation in 1910. Mutsuhito died in 1912 and his grandson Hiroito saw Japan lose this colony as a result of World War II.

One of the notable aspects of the Ravenna Effect in Japan, following the adoption of the capital Tokyo, was the diaspora. It does not compare in proportion to the 6th century BC Jewish diaspora, but it is difficult to imagine a country in the world today without the presence of Japanese families or their descendants.

Among the various wars in which Japan was involved during the period of consolidation of the new capital (let us remember that this takes 120 to 130 years) we can list: (a) I Sino-Japanese War (1894-1895), with victory of Japan, which incorporated the island of Taiwan; (b) Russo-Japanese War (1904-1905), with victory of Japan; (c) World War I (1917-1918), with Japan's victory with the Allies; (d) Russian Civil War (1918-1920), with defeat aside the White Army against Red Army troops; (e) Second Sino-Japanese War (1937-1945), with defeat of Japan; (f) World War II, with the defeat of Japan, along with its allies Germany, Italy, Hungary, Bulgaria and others; (g) Soviet-Japanese War (1945), with defeat of Japan.

Brazil received in 1908, in the port of Santos, the first ship of Japanese immigrants to the country, the Kasato Maru, with 781 passengers. It was the beginning of a series of family transfers, not only to Brazil, but to other countries in America and other continents. Many families from the United States came to Brazil as a result of the outbreak of the Civil War, most of them having formed the city of Americana, in Sao Paulo, but there is no comparison with the Japanese dispersal throughout the world in the first decades of the twentieth century.

With great technical competence, those responsible for the Japanese economy were able to control the high prices and the country was in a comfortable situation during the Great Depression, with an increase in GDP and an enhancement in the war industry. But the Ravenna Effect does not let anyone escape unharmed. In the 1940s, given the involvement in World War II and its conflicts with China, what historians note is that "inflation was rampant". Towards the end of the twentieth century, however, with the capital already consolidated, the country began to have very low rates of inflation, including a few years with negative rate.

Chapter 5 - Misfortunes

The three capitals we have just studied, with a brief history, have achieved consolidation after more than a century of suffering imposed on their peoples. The lessons learned from these vicissitudes are treasures for these countries. A few other capitals have gone through the harsh period of consolidation, but the vast majority of new capital experiences have resulted in resounding failure.

Let us look here at a list of misfortunes strongly related to the Ravenna Effect, that is to say, to the inflation of new capital.

Tutankhamen. Does a new capital leave anything positive?

In the year 1329 BC, King Tutankhaten ("Living Image of Aten"), at age 12, three years after being invested as a pharaoh, gave up the new capital, Aten, installed years earlier by his father, Akhenaten (formerly Amenhotep IV, or Amenofis IV), in the region of Amarna, and returned the seat of the empire to Thebes. He also gave up being Tutankhaten, name received as a tribute to god Aten (the Sun), and adopted the name Tutankhamen, honoring the god Amen, from the traditional polytheistic pantheon. He sounded the Egypt's finances and restored relations with other countries, which were shaken by the bellicose times of the new capital. But having General Horemheb as grand vizier, he could not avoid two wars in his short reign, one against Nubia, in the Nile Valley, and one against the peoples of the east. He died at age 19, most likely murdered because of palace intrigue, as historians speculate. Perhaps his death is related to the abandonment of the new capital, since the sources of misfortune always have their fanatical defenders.

The new capitals, despite the suffering of a dozen decades that they impose on their citizens, or their subjects, when not abandoned before consolidation, always leave something lasting, because they are built, or chosen, for the renewal of political methods, or customs. The case of the city of Akhenaten is recorded in history because of the great innovation it brought to the world: a monotheistic State. Many understand that Pharaoh took this idea out of his head, but there are those who research to prove another hypothesis, which is his living with the patriarch Joseph of Egypt, with whom he learned about the uniqueness of the Creator. If this is so, surely the notion of an abstract, purely spiritual deity was far from penetrating Aquenaton's understanding, but the novelty of monotheism delighted him. Then the phase of Aten, the Sun, as the only god took place.

Alexander. When did the glory of the city of Alexandria occur?

In the year 331 BC, Alexander the Great founded Alexandria, on the coast of Egypt, when he took the country of Darius III from Persia, and turned that ancient fishing village into the capital of his empire. There were 50 cities founded by him in the Old World being baptized with the name of Alexandria, but this one off the coast of Egypt was the main one.

In the year 323 BC, Alexander died, only 33 years old and eight years after founding his new capital. The empire was then divided between his three trusted generals. It was up to Ptolemy, soon called Ptolemy I, the part of the territory that contained Alexandria and there the new emperor built the *Museum*, which became the main research center of the time, and the famous *Alexandria Library*. As for the famous *Lighthouse* it was built under Ptolemy II, in the year 280 BC, by Sostratus of Cnidus. As is well known, the glory of the city, with its institutions, came in fact after its consolidation as capital in the following century.

Wars were a constant in Antiquity, and Alexander himself died in Mesopotamia on campaign. Thus, it is difficult today to specify how much misfortune for the Hellenic world in the first century of Alexandria came about through capitalnovism.

Antipas. What city did Herod Antipas have built in Galilee?

Son of Herod I, Herod Antipas was raised in Rome, alongside his brothers Herod Archelaus and Herod Philippus. At the death of Herod I, he was named by Caesar Augustus as tetrarch of Perea and Galilee. Leaving Jerusalem, he settled in Sepphoris, but in the year 20 built the city of Tiberias, on the shores of Lake Genezareth, which he renamed Lake Tiberias, named after Tiberius, the new Roman emperor.

It can be said that Herod Antipas was a clumsy man. To have a second marriage, he reneged on his wife, who was the daughter of the monarch of the Nabataean Kingdom, which is now Jordan and whose capital was Petra, also called Raqmu. This new marriage was with his sister-in-law Herodias, wife of his stepbrother Herod Plilip. The king of the Nabataeans, Aretas IV, felt disgraced and decided to attack the tetrarchy of Herod Antipas, but Lucius Vitellius, governor of Syria, intervened and avoided the end of Antipas.

Under his command perished John the Baptist, the Jordan River preacher, as recorded by historian Flavius Josephus.

With the death of Tiberius in the year 37 and the rise of Caligula, who was protector of Herod Agrippa, nephew of Antipas, Agrippa won from the new emperor the crown of Judea, south of Jerusalem. Antipas complained to Caligula, claiming that rightfully the crown of Judea belonged to him, Antipas. To defend himself Agrippa accused Antipas of establishing a secret alliance with the Kingdom of Parthia to fight Caligula. This one exiled Herod Antipas and his wife Herodias, in 39, sending them to the Pyrenees, where Antipas died that same year, and handed over the former Antipas crown to Agrippa, who became Herod Agrippa I. He reigned for five years. succeeded by Roman prosecutors, by determination of the new emperor, Claudius. It was then sworn in the prosecutor Cuspius Fadus, who was succeeded in the year 46 by Tiberius Julius Alexander. This one ruled Israel until the year 70, when Jeerusalem was destroyed by the Roman army and the Jews were scattered throughout the world for two millennia.

Most likely these events would have been avoided if Herod Antipas had reigned from his palace in Jerusalem, accepting the presence of the Roman governor Pontius Pilate. But he wanted to build a new capital. In the twentieth century, when the State of Israel was restored, the important and modern city of Tel Aviv was handed over to the Israelis as their capital. That would be fine if it weren't for the fact that Tel Aviv had no secular historical status of capital. Inflation has eroded the country. Jerusalem had been declared an international city, run by the UN. Involved in successive wars, the State of Israel took possession of Jerusalem in the 1967 battle, and solved its inflationary problem. Other major problems persist, as is known.

Honorius What historical fact occurred in Rome in the year 402?

In the year 476 the barbarians of Odoacer invaded the city of Rome. They were greeted with relief and even applause by the residents.

Rome had been suffering, since the year 402, problems of various shades, many of them new. In addition to the rampant dearness, many internal and external wars, often unusual, were plaguing the Romans and all the inhabitants of the Italic Peninsula.

The many provinces, such as the Iberian Peninsula, Syria, Romania, Gaul, and England, felt abandoned. Latinity did not reach its full end simply because of the papacy, which represented a link between all these peoples.

What had happened in the year 402, anyway? Emperor Honorius that year decided to set up the court in the small town of Ravenna.

From this year until the year 476, Rome could not sleep in peace. When the barbarians dominated Rome, they automatically took the empire for themselves. In Ravenna the Emperor that year was Romulus Augustus, who, for complete lack of ability to react, neutralized himself as an agent of power.

Once the location of the capitals in the history of the countries was considered unimportant, outside of Italy there is hardly any record of this Ravenna passage on the way to Rome. For almost all of the basic history books, the Fall of Rome, or Fall of the Roman Empire, occurred in the year 476, without reference to the fact that the city of Rome had been abandoned before.

Non-Italian students generally ignored the fact. Given this, this author, during a lecture to undergraduate students in the center of Sao Paulo, in 1993, about the role of Versailles and Weimar in the uncontrolled prices, risked the statement, as an exercise of confirmation by reciprocal movement, of that Rome, when it fell into the hands of the barbarians of Odoacer, did not house the emperor's residence. The students asked in which city the chief of State was then. This speaker could not answer, but recommended consulting a comprehensive encyclopedia (there were no internet search engines yet, not even Altavista, which only hit the market in 1995).

As soon as he returned home, the speaker consulted an encyclopedia and learned about Ravenna. The names Versailles Effect (by Prof. Malcolm Hewitt Wiener) and Weimar Effect (by Prof. Phillip David Kagan) already had established meanings in the academy, so this author had been using the expression Versailles-Weimar Effect. Taking note of Ravenna's oldest case, ir arose the idea of using Ravenna Effect came up. (*Versailles Effect*: The fashions and customs of a new sophisticated capital influence neighboring countries. *Weimar Effect*: Overinflation over the years has led to the gradual impoverishment of the middle class and the popular classes. *Ravenna Effect*: The installation of the residence of the chief of State in a city without a secular historical status of national capital provokes contempt for symbols, striking mainly the currency and creating inflationary impulse, or impulse of dearness. The other national heritage, also a symbol, to suffer deterioration, is the language, with successive breaks of the grammar rules.)

Zhao. What year was paper money invented?

Emperor Zhao Gou cannot be accused of having bad intuition when he left the old Chinese capital Kaifeng and moved to Hangzhou, in 1127. As Prince Don John did in 1808, sailing from Lisbon to Salvador, in the New World, to escape Napoleon's men and save the reign, likewise Zhao Gou, defeated in Kaifeng by Kublai Khan, grandson of Genghis Khan and last Khan of the Mongolian Empire, rushed to this new capital, Hangzhou, seeking to drive the reign from South China.

A little over a century earlier, unforeseen circumstances of trade and industry led to the creation of paper money in China.

We know that before the second millennium of our era began, the concept of currency was based on the understanding of the "it is worth as much as it weighs". For small values coins could be made of bronze, copper or other metals. Median values were traded in silver coins, while large sums demanded gold coins.

At the end of the first millennium, the province of Szechuan experienced a severe shortage of coins used for coinage. Someone came up with the idea of producing iron coins. It was a bad idea that later on required creativity to get the trade out of a complication. Iron was abundant, and the pieces used as currency were very heavy. The solution was the creation of the "money houses", a sort of registry office that functioned as a depository, issuing printed certificates representing the iron value that the subjects kept there. Gradually, the commerce began to accept the certificates, as if they were the iron coin itself.

Larcenists soon emerged, taking advantage of the good faith of their compatriots and trying to push certificates with values that had no ballast. Faced with many complaints, the government ordered the closure of the "money houses" in the year 1023.

However, the idea of carrying printed paper instead of heavy metals was very good, and in 1024 the government resumed the practice, no longer with the private business of "money houses" but with paper printed in a "national mint" belonging to the government. Since the government charges taxes, it can give ransom guarantees to those who carry paper money without major difficulties. This was the year in which for the first time in history society knew the fiduciary currency.

Historians and economists often claim that fiduciary currency did not prove to be an advantageous invention in the century of its creation, once it was soon attacked by inflation, but this is not true. For 104 years, until the installation of the new capital, the paper called *Chiao-Tzu* (exchange medium) worked properly and was good for Chinese. When Zhao Gou lost the war to Genghis Khan's grandson, this was due to factors other than his currency. It is almost certain that the Mongols had already incorporated the novelty. And, as we know, they were very strong, having dominated almost the entire Old World, from the Persian Gulf to the Japan Sea.

It was that century of tranquility with the Chiao-Tzu that made paper money return half a millennium later, in the Qing Dynasty, from 1644.

The Chiao-Tzu, under the new capital, has failed, as we now know it would, because of our knowledge of the Ravenna Effect. The philosopher Ye Shi (1150-1223) was the first scholar to write about the inflationary process, pointing out its ills on the economy of the country. By 1161, years before Ye Shi's complaints, the government was already realizing the depth of the problem. This year it replaced the Chiao-Tzu with the *Hui-Tzu* (means of control), a copper-backed paper currency. This was, because of inflation, the end of the fiduciary money, and the trauma lasted for centuries.

When the Qing Dynasty began in Beijing, in 1644, continuing until the proclamation of the Republic, in 1911, it replaced the Ming Dynasty, which had been in the city for two centuries. Thus, the return of the fiduciary currency was not at risk, because it was on safe ground, which was the consolidated capital.

Peter. Which emperor left St. Petersburg as capital?

The capital St. Petersburg, founded by Peter I of Russia, or Peter the Great, in 1703, functioned for a short time as a capital, bringing wars, famines, and other sufferings to the population at that time, until it was abandoned by his grandson, Emperor Peter. II, crowned in Moscow in 1728, at the age of 12, at the will of Empress Catherine I, second wife of Peter I and his successor.

Peter I was called The Great not so much for his deeds, but for his stature, which was 2.03 meters. And St. Petersburg earned its name not in honor of the founder, but because it was built around the former Peter and Paul Fortress, on Luga Bay, which is located in the Gulf of Finland.

Catherine I had 11 children with Peter, but all died in childhood, so Prince Alexis Petrovitch's firstborn, Peter, who became Peter II, was the only heir recognized by the Russians to succeed Catherine I, who reigned from 1725 to 1727, and she herself yielded to the appeals of the court and the population. The young man grew up in the care of his sister Natalia, because he was despised by his grandfather and by the empress.

Having spent part of his youth in the Netherlands as a shipyard worker, Peter I was the Tsar who modernized Russia, giving impetus to the shipping industry and leading the Russians to adopt Western European customs, both in politics and clothing, and various habits, although he could not in his day replace the old Julian calendar with the Gregorian calendar. However, it made the mistake of creating a new capital, although justifying its act as a need to facilitate and encourage maritime trade.

Antoinette. Did the French exempt Versailles from the great economic problem?

We dealt above with Colbert's possible influence on Louis XIV in the transfer of the French administration from Paris to Versailles, but we have not yet addressed the politically most turbulent phase of the human saga, the one that led scholars to divide History into the Modern Age, which had come since 1453, with the Fall of Constantinople, and Contemporary Age, begun in 1789, with the Fall of the Bastille.

The gradual and exponential weakening of the monarchy, due to its inability to solve the problems brought about by the Ravenna Effect, strongly affected the court of Louis XVI, leading him to cede more and more power to representatives of the bourgeoisie and the popular classes. The biggest victim of bullying during that period of fermentation of the French Revolution was the wife of the king, Marie Antoinette Josephe-Jeanne de Habsburg-Lorraine. While taking careful not to arouse monarchical sympathies in the young, historians, who have the newspapers as their substantial source of information, are reluctant to coldly analyze the relationship between the French bourgeoisie and the queen, suggesting so that all the faults attributed to her were well reasoned.

Fifteenth daughter of Emperor Francis I of Austria, Marie Antoinette married at the age of 14 with the dauphin of France, future King Louis XVI. As soon as she settled in Versailles, the French had for her a dishonorable nickname based on her nationality. Instead of calling her "l'austrichienne" (the Austrian), they called her ("l'autre chienne" (the other dog). Since she had no experience with a life of overwhelming dearness, her opinions on the economic moment were inconvenient. They gave her words she never uttered, but seemed credible given her position, such as the alleged response to the demand for bread, as a call for food: "If they have no bread, let them eat cake". Many rumors ran with aura of absolute truth, and this encouraged the creation of new rumors.

Her claim was to look after her garden in Versailles, but if the king was wrong to seek a solution to the country's serious economic problems, the explaining in the minds of the French was the influence of his foreign consort.

While trying aid in society to correct the economy, the king convened the session of the General States, in 1788. It was an assembly of three sectors, which were the nobility, the clergy, and the Third State, each with a third of the votes in the deliberations that the house would take. The Third State was the fraction that represented the bourgeoisie and the popular classes.

The inauguration of these representatives took place on May 5, 1789. In the first debates it was already present the dissatisfaction of the Third State, which, representing 98% of society, did not accept the quota of one third of the voting power, and also did not accept separate counting. It required that the votes be counted together, in the rule known as "one man one vote". The following month, nobility and clergy decided to reject that proposal, which led the Third State to declare itself National Assembly.

Louis XVI then locked the room where the sessions were held and the Third State began to meet in the sports court, the Ball Game Hall. Several representatives of the clergy and nobility adhered to the measure taken by the Third State, and the king finally accepted that the National Assembly should hold joint sessions.

On July 9, representatives of the three sectors, now meeting together, declared that the National Assembly would become the National Constituent Assembly, embarking on work that would last two years. Immediately, on July 10, the representatives declared the absolutist monarchy abolished, thus replaced it by the constitutional monarchy.

On the 13th the population dawned knowing that the government had authorized a 100% increase in the price of bread, among other readjustments. Then followed a tumultuous popular uprising. Louis XVI detached the state police to try to counter the revolt. The Assembly, in time, created a new police body called the National Guard, which also took action. Neither the executive nor the legislative police succeeded in controlling the situation.

On July 14th, 1879, the folk stormed the arms store at the Invalids Hotel, and from there they rushed to the Bastille Prison, where they thought they could stock up on ammunition. For that, they destroyed the prison, in action that became known as the "Fall of the Bastille". After that, Louis XVI ordered his soldiers to retreat.

On August 4th, the nobility's deputies agreed to abolish the perks of the aristocracy, such as the differentiated tax, the official tithing for clergy, and the reservation of vacancies in public jobs. On the same day the Assembly declared the society of privileges abolished, declaring the end of the *Ancient Regime*, but the king did not accept the document. So, the Assembly proceeded to draft the "Declaration of the Rights of Man and Citizen", which was voted and approved on August 26th. It determined the equality of all humans before the law, the right to property and security, the right to liberty, the principle of presumption of innocence, the principle of separation of powers and freedom of expression, among other guarantees.

From October 5th to October 6th, as noted above, it happened the "March of Women on Versailles", which after much negotiation and violent scenes brought the monarch and his wife to reside at the Tuileries Palace, in Paris.

The positive side of Marie Antoinette's presence and the entire campaign against her was precisely that of the surge of understanding that the economic and behavioral problems of France in those days were emanating from Versailles. Once it was only a feeling, with no concern for scientific approach, no general basis was established for this finding, so that the blame was restricted to the Palace of Versailles, with its tenant imported from Austria.

In the following months, France, by order of the Assembly, implemented numerous changes, such as the granting of the right of citizenship to Protestants, the end of the titles of nobility, the breaking of relations with the Pope and the Holy See, and the abolition of the corporations of office. .

As more than 300,000 family members of the nobility have left the country since the Fall of the Bastille, it was time for the emigration attempt also of the royal couple, which took place on the night of June 21st, 1791. However, Both were recognized in Varennes, arrested and returned to Paris. Mistrust of Marie Antoinette's role in this attempt to escape settled in the minds of the French.

In September the king signed the new constitution of France, making the new model of constitutional monarchy official.

The following year, on April 20th, Louis XVI signed a declaration of war on Austria, Bohemia and Hungary. Some historians record that he signed in tears the order of war against his father-in-law's country. But soon there was a rumor among the population that the war was a trap for Austria and other neighboring countries to enter the country to revoke the Revolution.

The "sans culotte" (the "no trousers") invaded the palace, prompting the royal couple to seek refuge in the Assembly. As a result, the royal family was imprisoned in the Temple Prison from August 13th, 1792. With the king arrested, the revolutionaries created the National Convention to function as Executive Branch. On September 21st the Republic was proclaimed.

In December, under the leadership of Robespierre, with Danton as minister of justice, the revolutionaries began the trial of Louis XVI, on charges of treason to the fatherland.

On January 21st, 1793, King Louis XVI and Queen Marie Antoinette were guillotined in Concorde Square.

The Convention was divided into two opposing wings: The Girondins, who sat on the right and were reticent about the advances of the Revolution, and the Jacobins, who sat on the left and wanted to move faster. Guillotines had been taking place encouraged by the differences between these two factions. After the death of the royal couple, that did not change.

Danton, who was sensible, began to complain about the large number of executions. Accused of corruption by his own high school classmate, Robespierre, he was guillotined on April 5th, 1794. It is said that before being placed under the blade, he said to Robespierre: "Today is me, tomorrow it is you."

Robespierre should not only be thought of as a killer, for he has played an important role in the economy. Once inflation, as far as we know today from Mario Henrique Simonsen's studies, has a strong inertial component, it does not go away on its own without any shock. Robespierre interrupted it in France with a device called the Law of the Maximum, or Law of the Maximum Price, a kind of market price freeze.

But it still sent enemies and former friends to the guillotine. Finally, in July, after being arrested with 20 Jacobin co-religionists, he was taken to the scaffold without trial. With his guillotine, the period which within the Revolution became known as the Kingdom of Terror was over. The guillotine continued to be used in France for death sentences for common crimes, as had been the purpose of its adoption in 1792. It was made obsolete in September 1981, with the abolition of the death penalty signed by President François Mitterrand.

Ebert. What justification has led Ebert to rule from Weimar?

By the strong determination of the inhabitants of the United States and Japan, their new capitals, Washington-DC (1800) and Tokyo (1869), after all the inevitable inconvenience they brought, were consolidated as the residence of their respective chiefs of State. This was not the case with the city of Weimar, which housed the German government from the beginning of 1919, after the end of the monarchy, with the abdication on November 9th, 1918, of Emperor William II, defeated in World War I. The successor of the last German emperor was President Friedrich Ebert, of the Social Democratic Party (SPD), who took office on February 4th, 1919, directing the country for six years, until he handed over to his successor Paul von Hindenburg in February 28th, 1925.

Since November 9th, 1918, the date of the end of the monarchy, Ebert had been holding the post of chancellor within the Republican provisional government, which in Germany is responsible for being prime minister. The parliamentary structure of the period was the People's Representatives Council

Unlike the kings of old dynasties, who were led by unsuspecting advisors, presidents in the modern republics made the decision to exchange the capital for willful whims, pressured in some cases by circumstances that served as subterfuge. This was the case of Friedrich Ebert, pushed into the abyss by the turmoil that followed the emperor's exile in the Netherlands, in the so-called "Christmas Riots".

Conservative currents demanded from Ebert, a center-left man, a transition to the Republic that, in the economic and social fields, maintained the status quo. The Spartacist League, led by the young Rosa Luxemburg and Karl Liebknecht, and several other segments linked to union struggles tried to pull the administration through popular demonstrations and strikes to join the line of the Russian Revolution.

On December 24th a group of communist militants seized one of the government buildings in Berlin.

With the explosion of Christmas Riots, resulting from a breakout in the streets, the head of government, under intense pressure, ordered a military action to return the order to the capital.

The result of the military repression was not the peace of mind, but the dissolution of the People's Council of Representatives, on December 29th, 1918.

The riots continued in early 1919 and amid the clashes a wing of the Spartacist League founded the German Communist Party (KPD).

This included Berlin police chief Emil Eichhorn, who was soon fired of his position. Eichhorn refused to leave the post and in his support the protesters intensified the protests, which led to an insurrection close to a civil war on January 8th, 9th and 10th.

To counter the crisis, the militias known as *Freikorps* (Free Bodies) joined the German army and, after defeating the leftist protesters, began the so-called *Battle of Berlin*, on the 12th, with attacks aimed at killing the known revolutionary leaders. On January 15th, Rosa Luxemburg and Karl Liebknecht were murdered.

These and many other deaths meant the government's victory over the insurrection, but more than that, it represented the rise of the hard line in leading the country. As fights were waged in the streets, Friedrich Ebert drew up the plan to abandon the old capital. This was done still during the days of clashes and murders, with the transfer of the main administrative bodies to Weimar, a small city, but of great cultural importance, having been the residence of poets the size of Schiller and Goethe.

On January 19th elections were held for Parliament, with the novelties of the female vote and the proportional system. The party that got the most seats was the SPD.

As already mentioned above, on February 4th the prime minister was sworn in as president and on 6th the elected parliamentarians took office, setting up the National Constituent Assembly, which on 11th confirmed Friedrich Ebert in the federal presidency. The aim was to create a modern Republic, free from the vices of the imperial times and the political bad habits cultivated in Berlin. Weimar would be the beginning of a new era for Germany.

It was all an illusion. Since we cannot overcome the law of gravity with a single leap, neither we can circumvent the limitations imposed on us by the laws of Social Psychology.

One may wonder why in Berlin there was the insurrection in the three weeks leading up to the transfer of Ebert's office to Weimar, if the Weimar Effect would come later. The answer is simple. Long before society has *resilience*, which is the ability to adapt to new situations without carrying deformations during the process, it has *hysteresis*. This means persistence of an effect caused by a source that has recently stopped emitting its energy flow. The idea comes from the electromagnet, which remains with magnetizing power moments after turning off the electricity that fed the piece.

In German society, the war ethos was very active under imperial power, as the world could see during World War I. The emperor's fall in November did not mean the immediate emptying of the warrior's mood, but maintained it for the following months, at least in December and January. From February 1919, and until November 1923, with the chief of State in Weimar, the great struggle of the Germans became another: how to survive under dearness and, sooner, under hyperinflation.

A long inflationary period weakens a society as much as a long war. While the war is heavily spent on armaments, ammunition and troop support, and deaths are due to enemy attacks, under prolonged inflation the country's resources are depleted in currency devaluation and deaths are caused by starvation and lack of money for medicines, all due to the widespread misery that makes up the phenomenon called the Weimar Effect, according to Professor Phillip David Kagan.

On April 4th, 1919, revolutionary groups overthrew the Bavarian state government and proclaimed a Soviet Republic there. Expropriations and executions were being carried out until in May the *Freikorps*, displaced from Berlin, arrived in Munich and dismissed the new rulers.

After approving the Treaty of Versailles at the end of June, the National Assembly closed the work on drafting the new Constitution, on July 31st. The Constitution was promulgated on August 11th.

On March 12th, 1920, the *Freikorps* unleashed a coup d'état in Berlin, declaring President Ebert deposed and raising Wolfgang Kapp to head of state. The federal government in Weimar called on the people to respond to the coup with demonstrations and strikes. After four days the coup was dealt with and its leaders fled the old capital. Ruhr Valley miners continued their strike, demanding high wages. Later they were accused of causing hyperinflation. Army units were sent there to end the strike.

On August 7th, the government sanctioned the National Disarmament Act, as provided for by the Versailles Treaty. The civilian population was called to report militia weapons deposits.

The value of the war indemnity was set by the London Commission on May 5th, 1921, at DEM 132 billion, or £ 6.6 billion, to be paid annually in 1.5 percent installments. The next day, probably as an answer, the German government signed an agreement with the Soviet Union recognizing the Communist Party as a legitimate organization to lead the Soviet government.

In September Adolf Hitler was arrested for participating in an attack on a Bavarian separatist and was sentenced to three months in prison.

Walter Rathenau, Foreign Minister, was assassinated in Berlin on June 27th, 1922, by members of the *Freikorps*. In July, Parliament passed the Republic Protection Act, outlawing groups that promised, promoted or committed murders or other acts of political violence.

Under hyperinflation the governments could not stand. In November 1922, Prime Minister Joseph Wirth resigned, being replaced by Wilhelm Cuno, a party man, without a party.

Wilhelm Cuno's office lasted until August 12th, 1923, when he resigned, defeated by countless wage replacement strikes, and was replaced by Gustav Stresemann, who took office with the support of the "Grand Coalition", formed by SPD, DVP, DDP and the Center Party. At the beginning of September a dollar was worth ten million marks. On October 1st, Major Bruchrucker, leading a group of the *Freikorps*, attempted a coup d'état in Brandenburg, called the "Kustrin Putsch", but official security forces acted swiftly and arrested the rebels.

On November 8th, the National Socialist Party of German Workers, under the leadership of Adolf Hitler, attempted a coup in Munich, Bavaria, the so-called the "Brewery Putsch". On the 9th, several participants were killed and Hitler was arrested. He was later sentenced to five years in prison, but was released with just over a year in prison.

If Weimar's hyperinflation played a role in the later rise of Nazism, it was to allow Hitler to try to seize power by force. Such a coup attempt would hardly have occurred under a stable currency regime. This upstart act of the Austrian began to build his fame among pro-dictatorship and anti-Semitic voters, including banker Hjalmar Schacht. With all the suffering caused by the hyperinflation that occurred within a social democratic management, it was easy for Hitler to climb into politics by attacking the social democracy.

Certainly Gustav Stresemann's rule would not last long. Also in November, on the 12th, banker Hjalmar Schacht was named president of the Central Bank, and on the 15th the bank launched a new currency, the Rentenmark, based on industrial productivity and sustained by the gold standard. A Rentenmark unit was worth at launch US$ 4.20.

The Schacht's measure came to abolish hyperinflation, but the SPD, the ruling coalition's main party, did not have the patience to wait for the results and on the 23rd withdrew support for the cabinet. On November 30th, 1923 Stresemann was replaced by Wilhelm Marx, of the Center Party, who in his role was center-right party. Since the government settled in Weimar, he has been the eighth premier, and has remained in office for a year and two months, overseeing monetary stabilization.

The year 1924 was relatively quiet for Ebert, because the new coin finally freed the Republic from a most oppressive fire test, which was hyperinflation. But the president was debilitated after facing many coup attempts, the most dangerous being the ultra-right *Freikorps* in Berlin; the ensuing major strike in the left-hand Ruhr Valley, which ended in assassinations of leaders and massacres, including the intervention of French troops; and that of Munich, led by Adolf Hitler, in Nazi-fascist action. Fascism, and its Nazi-fascist pup, are not right-wing policies that infiltrate left-wing groups, as many imagine. These movements are made up of leftist leaders, not aligned with the Leninist program, which has in the conquest and maintenance of power its reason for living and for this they persecute and massacre the communists, while joining the shabby-conservatism, which is the antiliberal-traditionalism. They proclaim a path that denies both bourgeois democracy (for Hitler, bourgeois social democracy and communism, as Mussolini wrote in his pamphlet "The Doctrine of Fascism."

In 134 times throughout his term, Ebert had to use his special powers to force rebellion and coup attempts. While suffering from gallstones and cholecystitis, he returned to Berlin for treatment. In the second week of February 1925 he was admitted to treat a severe flu, which could be pneumonia, but he contracted septicemia. On the 23rd he underwent an appendicitis surgery, but the infections got worse. He died on February 28th, 1925, being succeeded in the presidency by Marshal Paul von Hindenburg. Ebert's eldest son Friedrich Ebert Jr. was mayor of East Berlin from 1948 to 1967. Today, the SPD maintains the Friedrich Ebert Foundation, which upholds the president's legacy and is dedicated to the political formation of youth in the values of the social democracy.

Chiang. What economic situation paved the way for Mao Zedong?

After taking, with his nationalist army, the city of Nanjing, Chiang Kai-shek set up the headquarters of the Chinese government, starting the so-called Nanjing Decade, which lasted from 1928 to 1937. The city had once been the capital but had already lost its historical status. The year 1938 Chiang remained in Wuhan, the central region of the country. After that, from 1938 to 1944 the government was installed in Chongqing, in the southwest. From there it was transferred to Nanjing.

In 1941 Chiang Kai-Shek signed a peace agreement with Stalin, but this did not please the communist army, led by Mao Zedong.

After the end of World War II, nationalists and communists held talks in the fall of 1945 with a view to a peaceful arrangement to govern the country. Chiang was internationally recognized as China's chief of State, but Mao Zedong's group felt stronger. In 1948 Mao conquered several cities, advancing to Nanjing.

The high inflation that plagued China favored Mao Zedong's troops.

Chiang sought to secure possession of Taiwan, previously known as Island of Formosa, which Japan lost to China after being defeated in the world war. The occupation was not peaceful, with the nationalist army causing a massacre, killing about 20,000 people. After taking Nanjing, the communist army secured the inauguration of Mao Zedong, which took place on March 20th, 1949. As is well known, the new government settled in Beijing, the capital with a still-existing secular historical status.

Chiang Kai Shek ruled Taiwan as Nationalist China, from the island's capital, Taipei, for 26 years, dying on April 5th, 1975. During this period he was saddened to see the UN change in 1972 the representation of Taipei for Beijing, meaning that Mainland China, not Nationalist China, came to speak on behalf of the Chinese.

Tildy On the margins of which side did Tildy set up in 1946?

After a year-long First Republic at the end of World War I, Hungary restored the monarchy in March 1920, returning to the Republic only with the end of World War II. The president of that Second Republic was Zoltan Tildy, who led the country from February 2nd, 1946, to August 2nd, 1948.

While Friedrich Ebert installed the German presidential residence in a city without a secular historical capital status, Weimar, due to riots and deadly shocks in Berlin, and, for lack of knowledge, fermented a brutalizing hyperinflation, what happened in Hungary was more inescapable, an event of unparalleled misfortune, although it occurred in a much shorter term.

The Hungarian monarchy had been fighting in line with the axis, but in 1944 Miklos Horthy, Prince Regent, sensing the weakening of Nazism, sought to distance himself from the Germans, who no longer trusted him. In March 1944 the country was invaded by the German army, which imposed a new cabinet of government, controlled by a Hitler agent. A year later, on April 4th, 1945, the Soviet army expelled the Germans as a result of the so-called *Battle of Budapest*. The Nazis occupying the Hungarian capital were under orders from Hitler to practice scorched earth policy in case of imminent defeat, and they did so, destroying bridges, important buildings and all they could do, completing the damage done by the bombing of English and the North Americans in their attacks to aid the siege organized by the Soviets. With the Soviet army, a provisional government was then formed, headed by General Miklos. At the end of the year the Small Owners Party, headed by Zoltan Tildy, won the parliamentary elections. In early 1946 Tildy became president, officially abolishing the monarchy.

There was no whole house, no whole palace, no proper place where the president could stay overnight and maintain his office. Tildy then moved to a residence on the shores of Lake Balaton, the western and transdanubian region of the country.

In an attempt to save the war-battered economy, the central bank lent money at interest rates below inflation, which means negative interest rates in practice. If there was anything that posed no problem, it was liquidity: all demand for money was readily met.

The hyperinflationary process was rapid, reaching its peak in July 1946. The highest daily rate of inflationary growth in Weimar's acute phase of hyperinflation reached 20.9%, according to a survey by Cato Institute. In the Hungarian case, the (geometric) average daily inflation in July reached the rate of 207%. Inflation for the month was $4.19 \times 10E16\%$, the highest in the history of the world hitherto.

On August 1st, 1946, the Hungarian central bank, after dozens of zero-value cuts in the currency, launched a new currency, the florin, following the gold standard, and the highest inflation in history no longer plagued the population.

As for President Tildy, he had to resign his presidency on August 2nd, 1948, not because of hyperinflation, which he had long ago left behind, but because of family scandal. His son-in-law was arrested on charges of adultery and corruption. He returned to the government in 1956 as minister of State, but in the Soviet invasion he was arrested and sentenced to six years in June 1958. He served his sentence and withdrew from politics, dying in August 1961.

Mugabe. Where in Mugabe did you build your residence?

Killed on September 6th, 2019, at the age of 95, while this present book was being written, Robert Mugabe drove Zimbabwe for 37 years, from 1980 to 2017.

Military man, graduated in Letters and Economics, Catholic,

Mugabe was part of the group that fought for the country's independence. His dream for the emancipation of the country came from his youth, when he worked as a primary school teacher. He began in office as prime minister, but in 1987 was elevated to the presidency and unified the positions of premier and president, just as Hitler did in Germany in 1934. Unlike the Austrian, however, his struggle was anti-racist.

Mugabe as a young man militated in the Zimbabwe African National Union (Zanu), which was fighting for independence. He was arrested and sentenced to ten years in prison. After serving the sentence, he settled in Mozambique, while fighting for the independence of his country. It was at this stage, in the late 1970s, that he allied himself with armed groups who carried out attacks and sabotages against President Ian Smith's racist regime. Independence, however, came through an agreement signed in London on December 10th, 1979. For the following elections, the principle of "one man, one vote" would be in force, although white electors had secured a reserve guarantee of 20 % of seats in Parliament. Joined now to the Patriotic Front, forming the Zanu-PF Mugabe's Zanu obtained 71% of the seats. Mugabe became premier and Canaan Banana was sworn in as President of the Republic.

Despite being militant against racism, Mugabe had to manage, as prime minister, some ethnic wars between the country's most influential tribes. After abolishing parliamentarism and becoming president, from 1987 onwards, he ruled in relative tranquility until he made the "nouveau-riche" decision to abandon the old capital, Harare, and build a new administrative center and mansion to serve. as presidential residence.

In early 2006 the people of Zimbabwe took note of the president's capitalist intention, who ordered the construction of this set of works in Borrowdale Brooke, near Harare, to the north.

Market prices began their upward trajectory, and the citizens of the country related, as usual wherever such a new capital was set up, the rise in prices, and soon after inflation, to the large expenditures on those works. This false cause-and-effect relationship ceases a few years after the new administrative center is completed and construction costs are ended. Inflation and all the ills spilled over by the new capital continue to plague the population, and then the economic debacle gets a new alleged cause: the irresponsible impression of currency.

(🖐) Certainly, replenishing paper money through demand-driven printing is the cause of the rise in the inflation rate, but not the rise in prices. Without currency printing, prices will rise to the highest possible altitude, producing a situation of painful dearness.

In a short time the inflation rate reached the annual figure of 10,000%. To address this, the government has implemented an unemployment policy, leading to a rate of up to 80% of unemployed adults. It also tried desperately to control prices, imprisoning thousands of entrepreneurs.

In 2008, annual inflation was estimated to have reached 160,000%.

From the beginning of 2009 Mugabe undermined the high inflation with the adoption of foreign currencies, which began to circulate freely in the country.

One consequence of the period of hyperinflation was the return of parliamentarism.

In February 2009 he had to inaugurate Morgan Tsvangirai as prime minister. This one held a four-year term and, in 2013, Mugabe, already far from the hyperinflationary years, once again abolished the premier position.

On November 6th, 2017, Mugabe, now 93, dismissed the country's vice president, Emmerson Mnangagwa. The military and the population interpreted the act as an attempt by the president to pave the way to hand over power to his wife, Grace Mugabe. Days later he was warned by the Army that the Armed Forces would not tolerate the unjustified dismissal of leaders forged in the independence struggle. On the morning of November 15th, he and his wife were arrested, and he was forced to officially resign from the presidency. The vice president was elected as president, succeeding him. He supported the opposing candidate, Nelson Chamisa.

He passed away in 2019 unaware of the great good he did to the country by not giving up Borrowdale Brooke's presidential residence. He continued to live there, so President Emmerson Mnangagwa continued to reside in the old capital, Harare.

Records. Which country experienced the highest daily rate of inflation?

Following is a table listing the seven highest monthly inflation rates in world history, with the name of the country, the month of the national record, the index of the month and the daily rate within that month, in geometric mean. First, we must remember that Yugoslavia is on the table because its president, Marshal Tito, before his death in 1980, determined that the presidency of the country would be itinerant, traveling through the capitals of the federative units, leaving aside Belgrade, the traditional capital. The Serbian Republic of Krajina was just another victim of this decision. The case of Greece is similar to that of Hungary: The chief of State at the end of World War II was crowded on Crete because of the destruction the Nazis caused in the capital Athens. (The symbol "E" means "raised to".)

Country	Month	Rate%	Daily%
1 – Hungary	07-1946	4.19x10E16	207
2 – Zimbabwe	11-2008	7.96x10E10	98
3 – Yugoslavia	06-1994	3.13x10E6	64.6
4 – Krajina	06-1994	2.07x10E6	64.3
5 – Germany	12-1923	2.95x10E4	20.9
6 – Greece	12-1945	1.38x10E4	17.9
7 – China	05-1949	5.07x10E3	14.1

Recent. Which country announced in 2019 a capital exchange? The case of Borrowdale Broke, Zimbabwe, is not alone in the 21st century. Some other countries have swapped presidential residence at the end of the twentieth century or more recently, although the inflation they have caused has not risen to that of Robert Mugabe.

Countries with recent capital changes include Belize in Central America, which replaced Belize City for Belmopan (1970); Nigeria, which exchanged Lagos for Abuja (1991); and Myanmar, which exchanged Yangon for Naypyidaw (2005). Recently Tunisia also underwent a change of presidential residence. The president of the country changed the palace in Tunis, the traditional capital, to the old Carthage, which is officially a Tunisian neighborhood, but is 17 kilometers northwest of the capital, which has certainly been interpreted by Tunisians as a distinct Tunisian city. There began the so-called "Arab Spring", and the inhabitants of the country continue to suffer from high inflation.

While this book was being written, another closely related fact, such as Mugabe's death, occurred around the world: The Indonesian government announced on August 26th, 2019, that it would build a new capital, leaving Jakarta.

(✋) In his Political Treaty, Spinoza defined democracy as the regime in which the birth situation of the political agent does not matter. Indeed, the nouveau-riche ruler poses no problem, unless he decides to impose his iconoclastic sentiment on the traditional symbols of the country, which is a tragedy when the victim is the city of residence of the chief of State.

Chapter 6 - Rio

In 1960 Brazil "died on the beach" after much "swimming", warring and suffering. It is a very rare and absolutely unfortunate case what happened to the country that year. Certainly there is still a chance of applying a defibrillator that will bring it back to life, but arrogance and prejudice are almost insurmountable barriers to this perspective.

The colonial capital of Brazil was Salvador, since 1549. When Prince Regent Don John left Portugal in 1808, fleeing Napoleon Bonaparte's troops, he landed there in the Bahian Reconcavo. He signed the law of opening ports to friendly nations and created the Faculty of Medicine of Bahia. The administration of Brazilian territory, however, was no longer in that city. It had been transferred to Rio de Janeiro in 1763, 45 years ago, therefore. After one month, the court was moved to Guanabara Bay, but Rio was a capital without historical status. The arrival of the royal family in Rio triggered nine consecutive days of celebrations, once the event was immensely auspicious for Brazilians and for Cariocas in particular. Hard reality would come later.

Besides not being a consolidated capital for Brazil, the traditional capital of the kingdom was Lisbon. In Rio or Salvador, Don John would face serious problems.

Christopher. From whom did Don John win Quinta da Boa Vista?

The years spent in Rio were very difficult for Don John. There he became Don John VI, obtaining the king's crown after the death in 1816 of his mother, Queen Maria I, who had been suffering from mental problems for years. His older brother, Joseph, had already died.

Although aware that Rio, since 1808, had been the seat of a kingdom that extended to the four corners of the globe, the population did not respect the king, gradually mocking him. With the coming of Rio, it was concretized the proposal made by Father Antonio Vieira more than a century and a half earlier, to transfer the crown to America as part of a plan for the creation of the last and fifth empire of world history. Don John VI brought with him great European artists and scientists and installed in Rio lasting institutions that could be presented as the basis of a modern court and in line with the capitals of the most important countries in the world. But while in Portugal there was for many decades the idea of moving the court to Rio, Rio de Janeiro was not prepared for that. There was no palace worthy of receiving the

Braganza family. Given this, and showing enthusiasm to see his city housing the court, the merchant Elias Antonio Lopes gave Don John his site, in the north of the city, the Quinta da Boa Vista, which had a showy palace. Don John had some renovations and enlargements made before turning it into the royal residence, under the name of St. Christopher's Palace.

The economic problems soon increased. The attempt to take French Guiana from Bonaparte was unsuccessful. England, which helped Don John escape, imposed in 1810 a trade agreement that greatly damaged the Brazilian economy, which failed to develop its industry, in the face of imports of products of various types. The public deficit increased alarmingly, and the Banco do Brasil, which Don John created in 1808, went into crisis and was closed in 1829. It was to be recreated in 1851 by Baron of Maua.

Once in Europe these difficulties on the other side of the Atlantic were not known, when Napoleon was ousted, in 1815, the Congress of Vienna, in which the new organization of European states was discussed, Talleyrand and other diplomats recommended that Don John keep the court in Brazil.

Despite all the difficulties, Don John, as king, was able to take Montevideo in 1817, and in 1821 Uruguay was annexed to Brazil, under the name of Cisplatine Province. He also mobilized his diplomats to find a marriage for his son Peter, and in the year 1817 Peter married Maria Leopoldina of Austria. For this, the king expelled from Brazil the French Noemi Thierri, who was Peter's commoner girlfriend. That same year of 1817 the court had to face an attempt of dismemberment, the *Pernambuco Revolution*. Don John VI was beginning to lose authority.

Return. In what year did Dom João VI return to Portugal?

On August 20th, 1820, a military movement in Portugal installed a governing junta in the city of Porto, calling elections for representatives without consulting the king. The movement, called the *Liberal Revolution of Porto*, reached Lisbon and had repercussions in the Brazilian provinces of Pará and Bahia, also provoking military rebellion in Rio de Janeiro.

In Lisbon, a *Council of Regency* was formed, on January 30th, 1821, and this demanded the return of Don John VI to Portugal. Courtiers from Brazil disapproved of that demand, fearing that the country would return to colony status. But the Brazilian population was no longer satisfied with the royal presence in the country. On April 25th, Don John appointed Peter as Prince Regent of Brazil and left for Portugal.

On March 10th, 1826, Don John VI died in Lisbon, after suffering convulsions and fainting. Poisoning was suspected, but the cause of death could not be ascertained at the time. It was not until 2000 that a medical team analyzed parts of his body, which was exhumed for examination, and found that he was poisoned by arsenic.

After the king's death, Portugal demanded the return of Don Peter, who would be Don Peter IV, once Don Peter III was the father of Don John VI. Don John, feeling that his time had come, appointed his daughter Isabel Maria as regent princess. She remained in this condition for two years. The presumptive heir was admittedly Don Peter.

Independence

In Rio, by articulations of Princess Leopoldina and the politician and scientist Jose Bonifacio de Andrada e Silva, independence was assured, and Don Peter declared it, in Sao Paulo, on September 7th, 1822, becoming Emperor Don Peter I from Brazil.

If King Don John VI's life was not comfortable in Rio, neither would his son's life as chief of State.

Jose Bonifacio's plan for independence foresaw a political system based on the British model, in which Bonifacio himself would inaugurate the premier post. Don Peter I did not keep the word, imagining that acting as an absolutist monarch he would win his laurels for good administration. Intelligence and training did not lack him, for he had received education from competent preceptors. In Music, for example, his master was Marcos Antonio Portugal, an admired composer in all European countries, and with him he learned piano, guitar and flute, becoming a good composer of popular pieces. His work known to all Brazilians is the Anthem of Independence, with lyrics by journalist Evaristo da Veiga. But all the skill and preparedness of the chief of State descend into the abyss when his effective residence is a city without historical capital status.

Bonifacio obviously did not know the role of capitalnovism in leading the State, and attributed bad governance to the breach of the verbal agreement that Don Peter would have made with him, designing a constitutional monarchy for Brazil. "I have never met such a prince as Peter in his pusillanimity", he wrote in "Projects for Brazil".

The steps to independence are well known. Portuguese troops were sent to control the regency in Brazil. Peter gave in to those demands, but warned that this would be limited. After some political crises, an order came from Lisbon for Peter to leave. Fearing to return to the condition of colony, Brazilians organized a petition asking Peter not to answer his father's call. Eight thousand signatures were obtained, which were delivered to Peter on January 9th, 1822. In response the prince said: "As it is for the common good and general satisfaction of the nation, I am prepared. Tell the people that I stay!" Since then January 9th has been remembered in Brazil as "Staying's Day".

The Portuguese troops commander, Jorge de Avilez, tried to force Peter to leave. This one gathered troops formed only by Brazilians, who, with greater contingent, managed to surrender the Portuguese commander and he was sent back to Lisbon, accompanied by his soldiers.

In Sao Paulo, when he was with his guard in the Ipiranga neighborhood, coming from Santos, Don Peter received a letter from Portugal warning that Lisbon would not accept an autonomous government in Brazil. After reading the message, he uttered the declaration of independence, which ended with the cry "Independence or Death!"

The coronation took place in Rio de Janeiro on December 1st, but some provinces, distant from Sao Paulo and Rio de Janeiro, did not adhere peacefully to the new condition of the territory. In the year 1823 some battles took place in the South and other regions, with greater bloodshed in Maranhao and Bahia, in the struggles of Brazilians to expel the defenders of the colony condition to the country. These clashes led to the rupture of relations between Don Peter I and his main minister, Jose Bonifacio, because of power dispute. Shortly before the declaration of independence, Peter was admitted to Freemasonry. On October 7th, he became Grand Master of the Order, taking the place of Bonifacio. The emperor exonerated Bonifacio on charges of misconduct, basically because he thought he used his position to arrest some and expel other personal enemies from the country, some of whom enjoyed the friendship of the chief of State.

Elected to the Constituent National General Assembly, Jose Bonifacio denounced a great conspiracy against the interests of Brazil, and implicated the emperor himself as conniving. On November 12th, 1823, Dom Pedro dissolved the Assembly and instructed the Council of State to draw up a constitutional text, which he promulgated on March 25th, 1824.

Pernambuco. Which leader was hanged in Pernambuco in 1825? The first major conflict that arose as a result of the Constitution granted by the emperor was the *Confederation of the Equator*, an attempt to separate the province of Pernambuco, allied with Ceara and Paraíba. Since December 1823 Friar Caneca's newspaper *Typhis Pernambucano* had been criticizing the politics of the court, not only Bonifacio's office but the following. The dissolution of the Assembly and the imposition of the Constitution inflicted insurrection. With pamphletary writings inspired by European romantic intellectuals, the friar allied himself with physician Cipriano Barata and many other leaders in order to separate from Brazil the northeastern provinces. Professor of Rhetoric, Philosophy and Geometry, Joaquim da Silva Rabelo, Friar Caneca, from July 2nd, 1823, the date of the proclamation of the Confederation of the Equator, served as secretary of the rebel army and spiritual adviser of the separatists. But the forces of the empire, with the support of Admiral Cochrane, soon took Recife. Friar Caneca was arrested by imperial troops on November 29th and on December 18th he began his trial in a military commission chaired by Francisco de Lima e Silva, future Duke of Caxias.

On January 13th, 1825, Friar Caneca was hanged, followed by ten more rebel chiefs. Some of the leaders went into exile, hundreds of others were arrested, and the Northeast separation project ended at that time.

The following year, the Legislative General Assembly approved the creation of courses of Law, which were officially launched by Don Peter I on August 11th, 1827, for the city of Recife and the city of Sao Paulo. In the view of imperial power, Pernambuco, which had previously brought great wealth to the country through the sugar cane culture, was now dividing attention with Sao Paulo.

As stated above, after the death of Don John VI in Portugal, the throne was appointed for Don Peter. As he knew that neither Portuguese nor Brazilians would accept a reunification of the crowns, he named his firstborn Maria da Gloria, under the title of Maria II. Born in 1819 at the St. Christopher Palace of Rio de Janeiro, she was only seven years old. It was the only person born in Brazil to become chief of State on European soil.

On July 11th, 1828, Don Peter's brother Michael, shortly after receiving the position of regent, gave a coup d'état and crowned himself as King Michael I of Portugal.

Cisplatine. In what year did Brazil lose the Cisplatine Province?

Before that, shortly after the Pernambuco insurrection was over, Don Peter I had to face a similar problem in the South. Supported by Argentina, then the United Provinces of the Rio de la Plata, Uruguayan politicians declared Cisplastine independent, in April 1825. The emperor decided to travel. across the country to enlist soldiers for La Plata War. He went to Bahia, then headed south to Porto Alegre on December 7th, 1826. The war was on its way when he received the news that his wife Maria Leopoldina had died in Rio de Janeiro after suffering an involuntary abortion. Upon arriving in Rio, she was told that the empress had died as a result of assaults by her husband.

On August 25th, 1828, Uruguay declared its independence from Brazil and Don Peter I immediately recognized the defeat of the Brazilian troops.

Feeling guilty and sorry for confining his wife to the palace while traveling to the provinces alongside his mistress Domitila de Castro, the Marquise of Santos, expelled her from Rio de Janeiro, demanding her to return to the province of Sao Paulo, once she was from the city of Santos. Months later he accepted her back, but for a short time, once he found a bride, Princess Amelia of Beauhamais of Bavaria, whom he married in October 1829.

Recomposed to family tranquility, Peter began to think about his return to Lisbon, often referring to it. Advocate for freedom of expression and in favor of a plan for the gradual release of slaves, he was losing support among landowners and other conservative wings. He was often accused of not respecting the cabinet government, which would consolidate a constitutional monarchy. In March 1831 he showed that these fears were unfounded, as he inaugurated a cabinet of the formerly opposed Liberal party.

Abdication. In which city did Emperor Peter I settle on his return to Europe?

While knowing the emperor's desire to return to Lisbon, Portuguese residents in Rio caused a night of turmoil in the city, called the *Night of Garrafadas*. Days later Don Peter dismissed the cabinet, accusing him of acting ineffectively in the episode of the riots. The next day, April 6th, a crowd rallied in a public square demanding the restoration of the cabinet. Don Peter's reply was his letter of abdication on April 7th, 1831. He closed it with the words: "I retire to Europe and leave a country that I loved and still love."

In Europe Peter settled in Paris, where his wife Amelia had their first daughter, Maria Amelia, and from there he traveled to England and other countries seeking support for his attack on usurper Michael I, his brother. Without any title of nobility, nobody promised him help. He decided to resume the title of Duke of Braganza, which he sported before being emperor. When he met the Marquis de La Fayette in France, and received his support, his hopes were restored.

He returned to Portugal and began to organize the crown restoration army from the Azores Archipelago, the only Portuguese region that did not join Michael. From there, he landed in the city of Porto on July 9th, 1832, receiving the adhesion of the residents and valuable intellectuals.

Porto. What nickname did Dom Pedro IV have in Portugal?

Don Peter spent more than a year in Porto, strengthening his army and waiting for the moment to act. When he finally started the attack, he saw that the casualties on his side were greater than expected. Even so, he risked dividing the troops, causing some of them to attack from the south, in the Algarve region. The strategy worked, and the southern cities were not only conquered but they also provided contingents for his army. When he took Lisbon on July 24th, he thought the fight would end there, but was soon involved in a Spanish war. Don Charles, Don Peter's uncle, rose in struggle to take the crown from the hands of his niece Isabel II. Don Peter allied with the liberal armies of Spain that fought in favor of Isabel II and defeated Don Charles. A peace agreement was signed on May 16th, 1834.

Weeks later, Don Peter, now King Don Peter IV, nicknamed The Soldier King, fell ill with tuberculosis. He died in the Palace of Queluz on September 10th, leaving as heir of the throne her daughter Maria II, nicknamed The Educator.

While in Porto, busy organizing the attack on the restoration, he was visited by Antonio Carlos de Andrada e Silva, Bonifacio's brother. Brazil's political and economic situation, which was not good under Don Peter II, continued to deteriorate in the regency. His son Peter de Alcantara, who would later become Emperor Don Peter II, stayed in Rio when he was just over five years old when Dom Pedro I left for Portugal, naming Jose Bonifacio as the boy's tutor. The city was still a long way from acquiring historic status of capital, and the new rulers resented a more popularly recognized authority.

The former emperor of Brazil suspected that Antonio Carlos'

request came from a political wing, from conservatives who intended to consolidate power, not the population. He replied that he would only consider returning if the request was made by the Legislative General Assembly, with wide approval.

Considering that power was in fact established in Rio de Janeiro in 1808, the consolidation of the capital took place from 1928 onwards, after the 12 decades necessary for its maturation, with definitive guarantee in 1938. From 1763, the year of the establishment of the colonial administration in the city, the 12 decades were completed in 1883.

Ending the period of regency, Don Peter II was crowned emperor at the age of 15, on July 18th, 1841, after an ad hoc declaration of reduction of age, which should have been 18 years old, voted and approved in Parliament in July 26th, 1840, when he was therefore 14 years old.

Revolts

Several internal war conflicts took place in the country during the regency period. Among the most important are the *Cabanagem*, the *Males Revolt*, the *Sabinada*, the *Balaiada* and the *Farroupilha Revolution*.

The Cabanagem took place in Para, between 1835 and 1840. The local government, supported by an elite of European origin, was overthrown by a popular uprising formed by a contingent of indigenous and black people, the Cabanos, who declared the province independent. Troops loyal to the imperial government restored the former government.

The Males Revolt took place in the Reconcavo, Bahia, in 1835, and lasted only one day. Muslim slaves, the Males, who were literate, rose in rebellion to form the Male Bahia, which would be a country run by former slaves. The plan did not prosper and was defeated in less than 24 hours.

The Sabinada also took place in Bahia, between 1837 and 1838, led by Sabino Barroso, professor of the School of Medicine and journalist. Brazilian-born slaves who took up arms would gain freedom, as promised by the leaders of the revolt. Less than a year later the imperial troops recovered Salvador, Bahia's capital, ending the rebellion in a fight that resulted in over 1800 deaths.

The Balaiada took place in Maranhao, from 1838 to 1840, started in the south of the province by Francisco dos Anjos Ferreira, a basket ("balaio") vendor, who gathered a contingent of rebels to avenge his daughter's rape provoked by a police captain. Ferreira's group was joined by leader Cosme, commanding a group of 3,000 fugitive slaves. When the rebellion was defeated by the imperial power troops, leader Cosme was sentenced to death and executed in 1842, while the other leaders received amnesty conditional on the re-enslavement of the blacks who participated in the revolt.

The Farroupilha Revolution, also called the Farrapos War, took place in Rio Grande do Sul and Santa Catarina, from 1835 to 1845. By the closing date, we see that the authority of Don Peter II as emperor was not immediately imposed, needing four years to dominate the southern provinces. In September 1835 the revolutionaries proclaimed the Rio Grande Republic, and in 1837 they inaugurated as ruler the leader of the revolt, Bento Goncalves, who had Gomes Jardim as his successor. In Santa Catarina it was proclaimed the Julian Republic, led by Giuseppe Garibaldi. The adjective "Farrapo" (rag) was a derogatory term used by Brazilian conservatives to refer to liberals. Among liberals and republicans the expression became a source of pride for those who boasted it. The Farrapos War was the longest and most comprehensive of the internal rebellions of the Brazilian Empire. It was defeated on March 1st, 1845.

In the second year of his reign, Emperor Don Peter II had yet to face the Liberal Revolution of 1842, which occurred first in Sao Paulo and then in Minas Gerais.

Sorocaba. Que militar derrotou os rebeldes de Sorocaba?

At the time of the emperor's coronation and for the following months the Legislative General Assembly and the government were dominated by the conservatives. Tax hikes and retrograde laws had been displeasing liberals. The city of Sorocaba, in the interior of Sao Paulo, was the scene of protests, severely repressed. The city of Sao Paulo was not much larger than that of Sorocaba. Brigadier Rafael Tobias de Aguiar, who had already presided over the province of Sao Paulo for two periods, joined the rebels and led the rebellion, which was also supported by Father Diogo Antonio Feijo, who was a senator and had been regent until months ago. Sorocaba was declared provisional capital and Brigadier Tobias became president of the province. Feijo would take care of the government while Tobias commanded the fighting troops. While obtaining support from the cities of Itu, Itapetininga, Capivari and others, Tobias headed for the city of Sao Paulo to depose Jose da Costa

Carvalho, Baron de Monte Alegre, then official president of the province. The governor called for help from the war ministry, which sent troops commanded by General Luis Alves de Lima e Silva, Marquis de Caxias.

Caxias soon defeated the rebels. On June 13th he arrested Brigadier Tobias, who was trying to flee to Rio Grande do Sul, and the following week he seized Sorocaba and arrested Feijo. The two rebel leaders were taken to Rio de Janeiro.

Barbacena. Who was sworn in as president in the Barbacena revolt?

While Caxias struggled to defeat the rebels of the province of Sao Paulo, the province of Minas Gerais was following the footsteps of the revolts that were developing in the neighboring province and also in Santa Catarina and Rio Grande do Sul. On June 10th the city of Barbacena was declared provisional capital of Minas Gerais and Jose Feliciano Pinto Coelho da Cunha, who would later be Baron de Cocais, was sworn in as president.

As soon as Caxias dominated the province of Sao Paulo, he was sent to fight the rebels of Minas Gerais. His troops went through difficulties there, always intercepted by the revolutionaries. But he gave his brother Jose Joaquim de Lima e Silva Sobrinho the command of a detachment that followed another path, which may have been the result of a well-designed strategy. On August 20th the brother arrived in Barbacena and defeated the rebels. Teofilo Otoni, one of the leaders, and other commanders were sent to prison in Ouro Preto, then the provincial capital.

The rebels of Sorocaba and Barbacena received amnesty by the emperor in 1844, when the liberals, growing in political importance, took office in positions of the ministry.

The same politicians and courtiers who had anticipated the emperor's coming of age considered that a new step had to be taken for his authority to be respected. They found a bride for him, who married in Naples at age 17 with Theresa Christina, princess of the Kingdom of the Two Sicilies.

In July 1847, perhaps under the influence of his wife, Don Peter II definitively established the constitutional monarchy, naming Manuel Alves Branco, of the Liberal Party, as premier. The offices that followed, until the end of the Brazilian monarchy, in 1889, had little longevity, lasting an average of nine months, but the impression was that the governments were long and stable, thanks to the authority that the Emperor knew how to conquer and use. The Brazilian political model came to be seen internationally as an example of modernity.

The upward price trend was countered by the behavior of the chief of State. During the entire period of the second reign, from coronation to deposition, he refused every proposed adjustment to the maintenance allowance for the imperial family, which was 800 million reals a year. He dressed simply and rejected all forms of ostentation. Leap sonnetist, he spent his day at work and at night he read, studied, and sometimes wrote.

Praieira. Did Don Peter II give amnesty to the poor rebels of the Praieira Revolution?

Even so, a new internal conflict broke out in the early days. In the wake of the 1848 Revolution in France and several other European insurrections of the same year, Pernambuco lived, from 1848 to 1850, the *Praieira Revolution* (Beacher Revolution). The trigger for the revolt was the replacement of the provincial president, Antonio Pinto Chichorro da Gama, liberal, by the conservative Araujo Lima, an act interpreted by the Pernambucans as an arbitrariness of the emperor. Members and supporters of the Liberal Party gathered at the headquarters of the newspaper Diario Novo (New Daily), located at Rua da Praia (Beach Street), in Recife. It came from these activists, known as beachmen, the campaign for a revolution against court decisions. The revolution demanded total freedom of the press, the end of the post of life senator, universal suffrage, labor rights and reform of the judiciary, among other changes.

In 1850 a new president appointed for the province, Manuel Vieira Tosta, led by Imperial troops Brigadier Jose Joaquim Coelho, dominated the rebel troops in the battles of Agua Preta (Black Water) and Igaraçu (Tupi for Big Canoe). The leaders of the rebellion were tried and sentenced to prison in 1851. Later Don Peter II granted them amnesty. Some poorer revolutionaries had, however, been executed.

After this conflict, the cabinet regime secured several years of peace.

In 1862, had it not been for the emperor's balance and resilience, a major war could have taken place. Britain's Consul in Rio, William Dougal Christie, sought revenge on two episodes that occurred on the Brazilian coast that day. In one of them, a British ship wrecked in Rio Grande do Sul and its cargo was looted by popular. In the other, British officers landed in Rio and drunkenly rioted and were arrested. The consul gave orders to the British navy to capture Brazilian merchant ships in retaliation. Don Peter II ordered the Brazilian navy to resist any attack. The consul turned back, but the emperor severed diplomatic relations with London in 1863.

Paraguay. Which Argentine province was invaded by Solano Lopez?

At the end of 1864 the army of Brazil was involved in a Uruguayan conflict, where a civil war was taking place. This intervention soon overthrew President Bernardo Berro and imposed the inauguration of Venancio Flores. Taking advantage of this operation of the Brazilian troops, Paraguayan President Marechal Francisco Solano Lopez incorporated in December the province of Mato Grosso, an area that today is divided between the two states of Mato Grosso and Mato Grosso do Sul.

By the Treaty of Tordesillas, of 1494, the region of Mato Grosso did not belong to Portugal, but to Spain. Although it was revoked much later, the union of the Iberian crowns in 1580 rendered this treaty obsolete. In the decades that followed the bandeirantes entered the backlands founding villages and colonizing large tracts of the South American territory east of the Andes. Many Hispanic Americans imagine a diffuse right to these lands because of the Spanish ownership in those days, but the idea does not hold, because if the treaty were in force, Spain, not its former colonies, would own that region.

In April 1865 Paraguay also invaded the Argentine province of Corrientes. By the territorial pretensions of Solano Lopez, his country would have an area equivalent to Brazil, if not larger. From the beginning of 1965 Brazil was preparing to retake Mato Grosso. With the Paraguayan invasion of Argentina, Argentina and Uruguay allied with Brazil to form the Triple Alliance to fight the marshal. The *Paraguayan War* began there.

Solano Lopez, a military man of Spanish and Guarani indigenous offspring, when he organized the seizure of Mato Grosso and Corrientes was not yet a life dictator, but only a dictator project, once he had reached the presidency of his country in September 1862. Favorable narratives to his figure guarantee that the attack by the Triple Alliance was the work of England, which feared a hostile leadership in South America and used the South Atlantic countries to impose capitalism of English mould. However, it is known that the British government acted as the protector of Uruguay, having even worked for the country's independence, against the interests of the Brazilian Empire. And, as stated above, Brazil had severed diplomatic relations with Queen Victoria's domains in 1863.

Although he had only been a ruler for three years, that short time was enough to characterize the marshal's dictatorial intention. In any case, Brazilians lived under the monarchy, albeit constitutionally, and their capital still had no secular historical status. The warlike mood was latent, waiting only for a provocation.

The signal came with the invasion of Mato Grosso, which, according to Solano Lopez's preaching, was formerly Paraguayan territory. A ruthless massacre on Brazilian troops based in the province secured the Paraguayan yoke for a few years.

Don Peter II traveled to Rio Grande do Sul in order to organize the troops and make negotiations, contrary to the decision of the Council of State, which tried to prevent his personal participation in the war. He then declared himself a "volunteer patriot", obtaining in this way the adhesion of a legion of followers who accompanied him, also calling themselves "volunteer patriots".

In the Paraguayan attack on the city of Uruguaiana, Don Peter II was in the field and personally negotiated the surrender of the commander of the Paraguayan troops when they were defeated. This is where he received the English ambassador Edward Thornton, who proposed the resumption of relations.

There remained the question of the resumption of Mato Grosso, which was in charge of the new provincial president, General Couto de Magalhaes. In 1867 the general organized the Resumption of Corumba, succeeding and consolidating the rescue of the province.

The war continued until March 1ˢᵗ, 1870, when Solano Lopez and his son were killed in the Battle of Cerro Cora, northeast Paraguay. More than 50,000 Brazilians died during the almost seven years of the conflict. Politicians are said to have set aside money to erect an equestrian statue of the emperor to commemorate the victory, but he rejected the plan and determined that the money should be used to build primary schools.

Children. How many times did Isabel act as regent princess?

Of Peter's four children, the two boys, Afonso and Peter, died in childhood, and the girls, Isabel Cristina and Leopoldina Teresa, grew up healthy. There was no written Salic law, but its spirit was present among

114

the conservatives of the country, who did not welcome a successor woman in St. Christopher's Palace. Not only did they doubt the commanding ability of Princess Isabel, the eldest of the two heirs, but after her marriage they feared the interference of her husband, Louis Felipe Gaston de Orleans, the Count D'Eu, a French prince, even more so. after the fall of Napoleon III's empire, in 1870, with the consequent installation of the Republic in France.

Don Peter II had not prepared Isabel for State affairs. But he liked to travel, and during his absence from the country, when he went to Europe or North America on long stays, he named his daughter as regent princess. She has received this assignment three times in her life.

Abolition. Which journalist made the most incisive abolitionist campaign?

In the third and last of these regencies, Princess Isabel made a difficult decision that shook the relationship of trust between the conservative agrarian sectors and the court: She signed the law of abolition of slavery, the so-called *Golden Law*, on May 13th, 1888

Conservatives were hurt by the end of the labor system that had been sustaining the country's agrarian economy, and the liberals counted among their militants a large proportion of supporters of the republican regime. Upon returning from the trip, the emperor realized that the old balance that held him on the throne had been broken.

At that stage, slavery was a symbolic issue and only in appearance it continued to be a necessity in the country's economic relations, because several steps had already been taken towards the end of slavery. Prior to the Golden Law, the Slave Trade Ban Act, or the Eusébio de Queiroz Law, of 1850, had been approved by pressure from Britain, which had been demanding from Brazil a measure against slave trade. Another provision aimed at the gradual extinction of slavery was the Free Belly Law, or Viscount of Rio Branco Law, of 1871, declaring free all people born in Brazil from that date. And in 1885 the Saraiva-Cotegipe Law regulated the gradual extinction of the slave devices. In 1988, therefore, young Brazilians up to 17 years old were already free from slavery. In addition, the province of Ceara had already signed its abolition law in 1884.

In any case, this gradualism did not safeguard the most notable abolitionists, such as Jose do Patrocinio, Joaquim Nabuco, Paula Nei, Lopes Trovao, Aristides Lobo and Andre Reboucas. These wanted a definitive and comprehensive law, eliminating at once the scourge of slave labor.

The most important of the abolitionists was Jose do Patrocinio. Son of the parish priest of Campos dos Goitacazes and a slave, the mestizo as a young man graduated from Pharmacy, and at a later age became a journalist.

He began this phase of newspaper writer in early 1875, writing for fortnightly *Os Ferroes*. His pseudonym was Notus Ferrao, while his colleague, Dermeval da Fonseca, signed as Eurus Ferrao. From these fictitious last names came the name of the pediatrician.

This newspaper did not last long and in 1857 Sponsorship became a writer at Gazeta de Noticias, where he also subscribed to a column with a new pseudonym: Prudhome. It was as Prudhome that he began to spread the abolitionist campaign. In the early 1880s he bought the Gazeta da Tarde and then gave himself more fully to the cause of the slave's liberation. With Joaquim Nabuco and other colleagues he founded in 1880 the Brazilian Society Against Slavery and in 1883 created the Abolitionist Confederation, unifying there the various organs of the country that fought against slavery.

In 1886 he was elected councilor to the City Council of Rio de Janeiro, where he could amplify his abolitionist voice. In 1887, he finished the activities of the Gazeta de Noticias and founded a new newspaper, A Cidade do Rio, further intensifying the abolition campaign and gathering more prominent names in the new newsroom.

When on May 13th, 1888, Princess Isabel signed the law presented to Parliament by the Minister of Agriculture Rodrigo Augusto da Silva, who was a senator, Jose do Patrocinio, moved, climbed the podium and kissed the Regent's hand, a gesture soon followed by other intellectuals and abolitionists. The attitude was not welcomed by anti-slavery militants, who did not want a liberation negotiated with the court.

With the entry of the Golden Law into force, the greatest propagandist of abolition, which was Jose do Patrocínio, did not get the recognition deserved for his efforts over the years.

A little over a year later, the monarchy weakened, the emperor was overthrown by his trusted general, Marshal Deodoro da Fonseca, who had been invited by his Republican positivist friends to give a coup to topple the cabinet, which was premiered by the president Afonso Celso de Assis Figueiredo, Viscount of Ouro Preto,. The armed coup on November 15th, 1889, however, was intended to abolish the monarchical regime. The emperor was deposed and sent to France with his family, carrying a pillow full of Brazilian ground, to always sleep on the soil of his homeland, as he justified. Deodoro became the first president of the Republic of Brazil.

Jose do Patrocínio did not drown out his critical voice and in 1892 he caused displeasure to the new president, Marshal Floriano Peixoto. He was arrested and later confined in the city of Cucuí, State of Amazonas. The following year he returned to Rio on his own, but did not resume the publication of his newspaper.

From then on, he dedicated himself to monitoring the progress of balloon flights. In early 1905, when he was invited to salute in honor of Santos Dumont in the city of Rio, he suffered a sudden illness on stage, dying shortly after. His death occurred on January, 30th, at the age of 51.

Republic

From November 15th, 1889, until the coup d'état of October 3rd, 1930, Brazil lived what became known as the Old Republic.

As the titles of nobility were abolished, the republican government obtained capillarity in a country of mostly agrarian population through the National Guard colonels. They were usually farmers who bought this title and began to direct local politics. The vote for the Parliament was district, and this in Brazil came to be called "halter vote", because the colonels imposed on the poor to vote on the ballots with the names previously selected. In addition, they allowed access to the voter registration only to citizens who did not pose a risk of rebellion in the ballot box.

The constitutional rupture in 1930 shows that for Brazilians the recognition of Rio as a capital dates from 1808, in fact. The Great Depression, which was the 1929 crisis in the United States, had a major influence on the coup, but there was the domestic component, which was the unconsolidated capital.

In the Proclamation of the Republic, Deodoro da Fonseca was appointed president by the leaders of the overthrow of the monarchy, but the Constituent Assembly later elected him in a more "republican" way. The Constitution was promulgated in 1991, but the president resigned the same year and his deputy, Marshal Floriano Peixoto, took office as president. The new Constitution copied the political model in force in Mexico, from 1857, which had been an adaptation to the arrangement that elected in France in 1848 the romantic populist, Napoleon's nephew, Louis Napoleon Bonaparte, with the difference that in France the presidential term would be quadrennial, whereas

Mexico has opted for a five-year term. The system adopted in Mexico was consolidated only there, because in France itself, as we know, the president gave a coup d'état in 1851 to restore the monarchy, taking office as Emperor Napoleon III - the one who would be Napoleon II, Napoleon François, son of Napoleon Bonaparte and Maria Luisa, lived only 21 years and did not sit on any throne, although he received the title of King of Rome at birth.

The constituents of 1891 had as their presidential election options the United States system, by electoral college, and the Mexico system, by direct vote, which at the time was allowed only to male citizens. The Louis-Bonapartist model followed by the Mexicans was the chosen one. With a five-year term and direct election, since 1894, the presidents of the Old Republic were able to govern under relative stability, thanks to the tacit arrangement of the "coffee with milk" policy, which alternated a politician from the large State of Sao Paulo. coffee producer, and another of State of Minas Gerais, important for the production of dairy products. The agreement was interrupted with the "Revolution of 1930", which imposed a politician from Rio Grande do Sul as president, Getulio Dornelles Vargas, after preventing the inauguration of the elected president, Julio Prestes.

Following the mandates of the two marshals of the early republic, the following presidents have exercised government by direct election since 1894: Prudente de Moraes, Campos Sales, Rodrigues Alves, Afonso Pena (replaced by death after three years by Vice Nilo Pecanha), Marshal Hermes da Fonseca, Venceslau Bras, Rodrigues Alves (dead in 1918 by Spanish flu before taking office, being replaced by Vice Delfim Moreira), Epitacio Pessoa, Artur Bernardes and Washington Luís, who was overthrown in the end of his term in 1930.

New. What breakthrough did the 1934 Constitution bring to women?

When Getulio Vargas took office in 1930, setting up the provisional government of the 1930 Revolution, he hinted that the country would enter a new period of peace and progress. However, the political leaders of the State of Sao Paulo were not convinced of this perspective. In 1932, students of the College of Law protested in the center of the city of Sao Paulo against arbitrary actions of the federal government and were shot, four of them, Martins, Miragaia, Drusio, and Camargo, being killed. A fifth person, worker Alvarenga, was also killed later. The answer to this was the outbreak of the Sao Paulo Civil War, also called the War of 1932, or Constitutionalist Revolution.

Federal troops overcame the Sao Paulo rebels after many deaths between July and October, but the basic demand of the movement was met: a constituent assembly was set up in Rio in 1934. Among the significant advances made by the constitution that year was the voting rights for women. However, an attempted coup devised by the Brazilian Communist Party in 1937, although denounced beforehand and defeated, served as a pretext for the establishment of a fascist regime, chaired by Getulio Vargas himself. This one commissioned the lawyer Francisco Campos to draft a new Constitution, which was dubbed "Polish", and came into force for giving legal paints to an authoritarian regime, which received the name of *Estado Novo* (New State) .

The following year, 1938, the city of Rio gained, for all intents and purposes, its secular historical status as the national capital. The Vargas dictatorship took advantage of this and lasted until its incumbent's deposition on October 29, 1945, in the wake of the end of European Nazi fascist regimes. In the previous year, 1944, given popular pressure, after a Brazilian merchant ship was attacked by Nazis, the Brazilian government sent troops to Italy to fight the fascists and the Nazis. Getulio Vargas tried, therefore, to seek the side of the allies, but, as with other chiefs of State around the world, the "regret" did not convince the political leaders, and his deposition was inevitable. In 1946, a constituent assembly promulgated a new constitution, reaffirming the five-year term and the direct election of president. As for the general population, forgiveness was granted, for in late 1950 he was elected to the presidency by direct popular vote. He then ruled from January 31st, 1951, to August 24th, 1954, when he committed suicide amid clashes with the opposition.

Stability. What fact of 1960 led Brazil astray?

This phase in which the 1946 Constitution was in force was very auspicious, once the national capital was consolidated. The political problem was the insistence on copying the Mexican model, which led to the direct election of former dictator Getulio Vargas and the consequent governance crisis he would face. If it were not for this romantic option, the country would have greater international recognition than the one enjoyed in the Second Empire. In the late 1940s great works of great value were acquired from Europe and brought to the Art Museum of Sao Paulo, founded in 1947. Large numbers of immigrants from Europe and Asia arrived in Brazil, trusting in the great possibilities that the country offered. A Japanese householder, responding in the 21st century to why he chose Brazil to live in after World War II, said: "Brazil was the most promising country in the world".

This understanding was reversed on April 21st, 1960, with the inauguration of the new capital, Brasilia, by President Juscelino Kubitschek.

Dearness. What kind of coin did Brasilia inflation destroy?

When the actual construction of the new city began, in 1958, destructive signs began to appear. Prior to the 21st century, independent Brazil lived, therefore, only two decades under a healthy capital, from 1938 to 1958. It is not necessary to make the official change for the brutal occurrences of the Weimar Effect to surface. The decision and the guarantee that the consolidated capital will really be abandoned by the chief of State is sufficient. Just as in the 21st century with Roberto Mugabe, accused of causing a crisis in Zimbabwe because of the high expenses of his new administrative center, in Brazil they accused Kubitschek of provoking a general dearness because of the expenses with the construction of Brasilia. The gullible asserted that as soon as the construction was completed, the scarcity, as well as the inflation, which had picked up, would be a thing of the past. It was a self-deception.

Small coins minted during the reign of Don Peter II still circulated in the market in 1958. With them the children bought chocolates and fruits. In a very short time inflation has turned them into a museum piece, with no value other than that of memory.

(✍) When in inflationary regimes wages are adjusted, thanks to the printing of currency, workers gain a short period of relative financial slack. Soon after prices receive a new bullish momentum, bringing another phase of dearness. Thus, the dearness is embedded in the inflation process.

Military. What allowed Brazilians to live with long-lasting inflation?

Three years after the inauguration of the city of Brasilia, annual inflation reached the 100% mark under the Joao Goulart administration, and in the fourth year a coup disguised as zeal for public affairs, on April 1st, resulted in a military regime started. on April 15th, 1964, and ended 21 years later, on March 15th, 1985. The succeeding generals in the presidency continued to practice five-year terms, except for the last of them, Joao Batista Figueiredo, who ruled for six years. The commanding generals before Figueiredo were Castello Branco, Costa e Silva, Garrastazu Medici and Ernesto Geisel.

The surrender of the government to the military took place in the context of the Cold War, months after the assassination of John Fitzgerald Kennedy, as we saw above, but this olive period would hardly have happened in Brazil had it not been for the high inflation, which was playing the population against the civil government.

While Germany had three years of hyperinflation and Hungary had one year, Brazil and South America, under the influence of the new capital Brasilia, became a laboratory of human resistance within an economic tragedy for several decades. The reason was the mechanisms of coexistence with the currency deterioration invented by Brazilian economists. This fact caught Milton Friedman's attention and what he observed of the evolution of Brazilian inflation gave him subsidies to redo the Phillips Curve, which empirically related inflation index and unemployment rate.

Albeit in the face of all the suffering caused by Brazilian inflation, it was not planned to install the gold standard, even at the time it was officially in force in the United States, until August 1971. Castello Branco launched a campaign for families to donate gold to the government, called "gold for the good of Brazil", and perhaps there was a secret intention to embrace the gold standard, but it was never disclosed. The great strategy developed by the country's economists at the time, led by Eugenio Gudin, Otavio Bulhoes, Roberto Campos, and Mario Henrique Simonsen, was to link the currency in circulation to treasury bills and tax units. When Simonsen became finance minister, under the Geisel government, a sure impact measure was the use of the wheat subsidy. This impacted on food prices in general, serving to hold back inflation. By the end of the Medici government in March 1974, annual inflation had been lowered to 13 percent. Obviously it tended to grow rapidly, but price controls and the wheat subsidy prevented an explosion of the index, so that by taking over the successor, in March 1979, annual inflation had been 40 percent. Under the last president general, it was an impulse, reaching 240% at the end of that term.

Civil. What plan did President Sarney launch against inflation in 1986?

Jose Sarney, Figueiredo's civilian successor, who took office as vice in place of the titleholder Tancredo Neves, who, sick, would die a month later, had the central purpose of his term the fight against inflation. In February 1986 he launched the Cruzado Plan, with the introduction of a new currency, the Cruzado, accompanied by a total price freeze. After nearly a year of joy and monetary stability, Brazilians saw the plan fade as the government announced tax increases and controlled price increases for some products. The dammed inflationary impulse resumed its course. Other plans were implemented under the Sarney administration, but to no great effect. In his last month in office, from February to March 1990, the monthly index reached 82.39%. This value, if annualized, would have resulted in 135,422.8%. The next government, by Fernando Affonso Collor de Mello, applied a new price freeze and hijacked bank deposits that exceeded the equivalent of US$ 50 for 18 months. Once this plan also failed, he was deposed by impeachment in September 1992. When he realized that the open vote in Parliament would lead to his ouster, he resigned from office. The successor, his vice Itamar Franco, implemented in July 1994 a more consistent stabilization plan, the Real Plan, which did not abolish inflation but brought it to low levels, finally in the single digit range, i. e., below 10% per year.

With the apparent stability brought about by the Real Plan, Brazilians could breathe with some relief. The presidential terms, by amendment of the Constitution, became four years, from the successor of Itamar Franco. The success of the new currency, the Real, the same of the Second Reign, a constitutional amendment that has been much questioned by the opposition to the government, has abolished the ban on presidential reelection, allowing now one reelection for four years more. Three consecutive presidents were reelected, but the third of these cases, President Dilma Rousseff, was impeached a year and a half after the second term of office began.

Interest. What overthrew Dilma Rousseff in practice?

Officially, Rousseff's downfall came because she practiced legal accounting tricks that the law vetoed, making official banks lend to the treasury to camouflage a public deficit. In practice, the deposition was one more caused by inflation, as were Joao Goulart and Fernando Collor.

Towards the end of her first term, the president firmly believed that the inflationary impulse had been extinguished in Brazil, once the Real continued to have low inflation. She and her finance minister decided to risk high flights. First, the austerity that maintained a certain level of unemployment and a tightening of credit, preventing the industry from growing, as occurred in the year of the Cruzado Plan, was abandoned. Employment and consumption have been steadily increased. But there was a scorpion lurking, and this was the fall in the interest rate. Without much concern for macroeconomic fundamentals, she and her minister pressured the Central Bank to lower interest rates recklessly. Certainly, the government needed lower interest rates to pay lower public debt servicing, and the rate had been falling steadily. At one point, by the end of 2013, the reduction exceeded the critical level for that conjuncture. Already in early 2014 major popular demonstrations took to the street in the country in protests against price increases. In November she was able to obtain reelection, by small margin, but her political situation was already very precarious. Her second term was not sustained.

Even though historians, politicians, and columnists abstract the role of inflation in these events, the knowledge that was established was that the stabilization plan signed by President Itamar Franco in 1994 represented a downturn in the process of rising prices, but it did not abolish the inflationary impulse. It continued to sleep, never dying, and occasionally woke up, though suffering from dizziness.

The anchor imposed on the Real Plan was not only one. It draws on a set of anchors whose roles can alternate in the work of support. These anchors are unemployment, importation, confidence, interest rate, domestic industry breakdown and credit constraint. All of this is capable of keeping inflation at low rates, but at the cost of the country's development bottleneck.

Such action has not been taken in Venezuela, which suffers suffocatingly from the influence of the *nouveau-richisme* of the presidential circle from Brasilia. The IMF (International Monetary Fund) estimated 2019 inflation reached the annualized figure of 10 million per cent. In Argentina, too, inflation increased again in the first half of 2019, albeit at a much lower level than Venezuelan.

As with Rome, which deteriorated enormously in the 74 years in which the chief of State was in Ravenna, so did Rio in relation to Brasilia. The rise in poverty and violence in the rejected city has become a worldwide concern, undermining tourism and bringing astonishment to those who tried to give it the old reputation of being a "wonderful city".

Bossa nova, a popular rhythm that was born in Rio shortly before the change of the capital, was the last major cultural product emanating from Brazil to gain a world in the twentieth century. Lieutenant Colonel of the Minas Gerais Military Police, President Juscelino Kubitschek, who left Rio in exchange for a capital built in the middle of the Brazilian Plateau, earned the nickname "president bossa nova" from those who saw in his *nouveau-riche* arrogance some positive legacy for the country. Those who saw him stripped of his populist aura, disregarding the "office liturgy", of Jose Sarney's expression, have always known that he is part of the gallery of superb ignorant persons where Akhenaten, Herodes Antipa, Honorio and Mugabe live. There was nothing about him like bossa nova, and it is highly unlikely that he had sung *Road of the Sun* or *No More Blues* even during the bath.

Exits What lesson can we draw from Bonn's example as capital?

In every process of social corrosion there is some positive point, which lies at least in learning, in the lesson drawn from the mistakes made. In the case of the presidential residence in Brasilia, there was a significant gain amid all the suffering caused by persistent debacle: The arrogance of commanders was short-lived. Presidents clung to the office because they were paid a high salary in a country impoverished by the perennial Weimar Effect, but their lies and fanciful promises were hardly credible in the eyes of citizens. If two presidents in a row at the turn of the twentieth to the twenty-first century succeeded in two full four-year terms, totaling 16 years in power, this was because the Royal Plan signed by President Itamar Franco had the power to effectively tame the inflationary impulse, including leading a lady president to believe deeply in the invincibility of the measure, what made her lose the post. However, outside the gold standard, which has served for many decades as a mechanism to hold the dam, there are solutions.

It has been known since 1993 that the Weimar Effect can be neutralized by the *Bonn Effect*. Since the city of Berlin was divided between pro-Soviet and pro-American, at the end of World War II, the Germans on the western side, as it did at the end of World War I, this time because of the riots in the capital, had to transfer the federal administration to another city. They chose the city of Bonn. The big difference this time is that there was already the hard lesson about moving the chief of State to capital without secular historical status. In the years when the government was in Bonn, until reunification came on October 3, 1990, many problems were faced by Federal Germany, but among them was not the high inflation, which had been left behind in the days of the presidency. in Weimar.

The reason is that the administration was installed in Bonn, including the premier's residence, but the presidential residence was maintained in Berlin. No turmoil, no division required by Moscow, not even a threat of fanatics, none of this would take from the Germans the conviction that the right place to house the federal president's home was the former capital, Berlin.

What is done is done, as Pontius Pilate said. Brasilia was erected and became a megalopolis. The federal administration of Brazil has been accommodated there, and does not need to be relocated. However, keeping there the residence of the chief of State is pure insanity. If the country has any political learning capacity, it will never accept that the President of the Republic resides outside Rio during his term. (As "truth has not an only way", as Charles Sanders Peirce put it, another possibility can be tried, and this is the installation of the rotating presidency of South America in Rio as a confederation. Mercosur presidency, which needs to rapidly incorporate the Andean states, starting with Colombia and Peru.)

Correction. How to correct the huge income discrepancy in Brazil?

If Weimar's hyperinflation in three years has caused serious impoverishment of German families, especially the less well-off, it is not necessary to imagine the seriousness of the social disparity in Brazil between the highest earning, for income and salary estates, and the population of the lower salary ranges. The distance became almost abyssal, because for decades the owners were able to preserve their wealth, while the dispossessed watched their salary to fall month by month, eroded by inflation.

Chapter 7 - Peace

War is a psychosocial pathology. The diseases of the body, which are almost always caused by viruses or bacteria, are combated with medicines that attack these microorganisms or that act on the damaged parts, repairing them. So that the heal can be deliberate and efficient, the etiology must first be identified. This also occurs with psychic illnesses, but rather than exterminating microorganisms or repairing damaged tissues, healing occurs through drugs that regulate hormone production by the endocrine system or by blocking causes.

If some unwanted behavior arises out of motivation through some form of persuasion, or even self-conviction, then there is not a cause to be ruled out, but a problem to be faced with the use of arguments.

Doctrines. Liberal right can equal fascism?

In social life the political and economic conflicts are motives for endless clashes, which are as healthy as the degree of civility involved. In general the antagonistic fields are conservatism and progressivism.

Nowadays, social progression, which coincides with advanced liberalism, advocates:

1) full employment,

2) labor guarantees,

3) quality public education,

4) non-privatization of public services,

5) democracy (rule of law, periodic vote, non-longevity of the boss).

The liberal-democratic (**LD**) accepts these five achievements of the social progressive (**SP**), but demands that as few taxes as possible be instituted.

The liberal-conservative (**LC**) demands minimal taxation, even if items of social progressivism are sacrificed. The antiliberal-traditionalist (**AT**), on the other hand, is an individual who considers himself above the law and does not accept any of those five items. The plebiscitarian-populists (**PP**) defend the five items and others as long as they represent the manifest desire of the masses. The authoritarian-collectivists (**AC**), opposed to antiliberal-traditionalism and its neighbors in the circle of political doctrines, fall into two categories: one that continues to fight as opposition indefinitely and one that allies with the antiliberal-traditionalism to govern as fascist. A fascist, contrary to what was taught until the beginning of the 21st century to young people in South America, is not a rightist by formation, but a former authoritarian leftist. As a former leftist, he is not a leftist, nor is he a rightist. A rightist by formation is troubled when he is confused with an antiliberal-traditionalist or fascist, for he is a liberal-conservative, someone who rejects ideas of Thomas Morus, Stuart Mill and Umberto Eco, but cultivates concepts of John Locke, Adam Smith, and Alexis de Tocqueville. Labelling someone of the liberal right as a fascist is a demonstration of deformed reading or absence of political reading.

Since there is no effective political center position, whenever a person or party claims to profess a doctrinal center position, it is either center-right or center-left. So there are only six policy options. Thematic groups, such as environmentalists, ruralists, vegetarians, sex libertarians and atheist militants, need to take shelter in the parties representing those political lines, without creating their own party groups, once they serve to blur the electorate's understanding.

While following the presentation scheme of Jules Borely ("Le Nouveau Système Électoral", 1870), although the names of the parties will not be these, we have for the political-doctrinal spectrum the following disposition:

Liberal-Democratic   *Social-Progressive*

Liberal-Conservative   *Plebiscitarian-Populist*

Antiliberal-Traditionalist   *Authoritarian-Collectivist*

It is important to unlink both the identity demand and the customs agenda from the conservative-progressive classification. In the 21st century, advocates of the status quo began this deliberate confusion with the aim of diverting the focus of the political debate. Partisan programs should include the most favorable or least favorable view of sustainable development, because this is at the heart of humanity's progress for decades to come. Already discussing olfactory, taste or sexual preferences is part of another ground. Emperor Julius Caesar's sexual choice does not serve to characterize his political position, although it may direct his conduct in society.

In the strict ambit of politics as an attitude towards public affairs, societies that live under a democratic regime usually have an 18% proportion of anti-liberal voters, a number that comes from empirical findings. If the sectors that cherish the rule of law always have the necessary precaution, that 18 per cent will not have the political base to form government. If they succeed, it is because the democratic system is experiencing a crisis or because the other 82% relied too much on chance. When Hitler was elected in 1932 with 32% of the seats, he was 14% higher than that proportion of 18%, but this happened for two main reasons: First, he received the support of the great national hero, the monetary stabilizer Hjalmar Schacht, and, secondly, there was no prior democratic experience of choosing a political proposal as misleading as that of Nazism, with regard to the sale of pig in a poke. This second reason was behind President Hindenburg's impossibility to unite against Hitler the occupants of the remaining 62% seats and also behind the 88% support that the Germans gave in the plebiscite of the fanatic's rise to the federal presidency, which embedded the abolition of parliamentarism. Many see the Weimar Effect, which was the election of 28 separate parties to Parliament, whereas the proponent of the proportional voting, Jules Borely, wrote in 1870 that the maximum number of competing parties should be seven. This party dispersion, however, was just one more factor complicating and making the presidential plan unfeasible.

The main concern of the advocates of social democracy should not be with anti-liberal traditionalism, once it is easily identifiable, and believes in its own discourse, without the need for doctrinal camouflage. Everyone knew what the *Freikorps* proposal was, for example. If they end up alone, they are isolated and always in absolutely minority quantity. What should occupy the attention of the social democratic citizen is the infantile left, which permeates both social progressivism and ultra-leftism.

Unlike what occurs in front of the antiliberal-traditionalist, it is much more difficult to identify the agent of the infantile left, which is a potential fifth column of the democratic struggles. One must pay attention to the following signs, which he invariably presents: 1) rejects *negotiation* with democratic-liberals, betting on "all or nothing"; 2) imagines himself the only holder of the historical truth; 3) labels as imbecile those who do not accept their proposals; 4) believes in the conservative guess that imagines *hate* as the engine of political and economic decisions; 5) lives in a virtual *cave*, even knowing the ideas of the opponents; 6) is always susceptible to embrace *conspiracy* theories; 7) solemnly ignores that the opposite of healthy competition is the oppressive *monopoly*; 8) supports the *perpetuation* of the ruler that he deems progressive; 9) preaches that democracy means *direct* popular vote in the federal president; 10) advocates the expansion of free public services, but personally prefers to use *private* services.

It was because of that first all-or-nothing feature that President Hindenburg failed to form a majority against Hitler. And it was for the same reason that the UN failed to create, according to the purpose of the British chancellery, a Palestinian State, neighbor to the State of Israel, in 1948. The Palestinian Arabs, reinforced and pressured by the movements of their anti-Jewish neighbors, signed the position that they would only accept a State if it was their own, without dividing the territory with Israel.

A young politician may find that social democracy, so reviled by Adolf Hitler, is insufficient to emancipate the salaried citizen in the medium or long term. He is mistaken. Guaranteeing full employment and public education, things which social democracy can provide, if it is not sabotaged, leads to long-term emancipation. Good fruits are harvested after ripe.

Triad

Nothing in those political options (**AT**, **LC**, **LD**, **SP**, **PP**, and **AC**) is a cause of war. Political differences are used only as motivations, because the only causes of war conflicts are exactly the three presented in this text, which are:

    1 - Lifelongness (**L**),

    2 - Theocracy (**T**), and

    3 - Capitalnovism (**C**).

Those struggling on the battlefield are imbued with blind obedience and worship of the supreme chief (*lifelongness*), absolute belief in the need to destroy the source of sin that comes from their unfaithful enemies (*theocracy*) or revolt against those who, by iconoclasm or mere contempt for traditional symbols, tear apart the constitutive tissue of the social relations by submitting themselves to the influence of a chief of State residing outside the city that holds the secular historical status of the country's headquarters (*capitalnovism*). In the first and most comprehensive case, the one of lifelongness, the flag raised by the generals, whether ethnic, economic, territorial, moral, does not matter, for it serves only as a motivational element.

(✌) Causes, in the understanding of Psychology, are factors that generate pulsions, while motivations are just incentives. These can be undone through diplomacy and argumentation. Causes, by contrast, only cease to have their effect when effectively removed.

The direct election of president in the federal republic is not a cause of war, but of misery and mediocrity. Envy of ragamuffins in front of wage earners or owners (class conflict) can lead to theft, robbery and personal assault, but neither it can be cause of war, although it can be incorporated as a flag.

In any case, to build not only peace, but also social progress, countries must avoid:

I) Direct election of federal chief of State;

II) Unemployment;

III) Non-vocational high school;

IV) Food stamps for those who can work;

V). Monopolies - and, in bids, collusions (consortia).

An effective monopoly elimination policy provides gains in 1) *cost*, 2) *innovation*, 3) *attendance*, 4) *expansion*, 5) *fairness*, 6) *enthusiasm*, and 7) *quality*. Even state-owned enterprises should be set up as monopolies.

Systematic unemployment is also something that needs to be seen as a scandalous thing in big cities, since Keynes's book on the subject, *General Theory of Employment, Interest and Money*, was published many decades ago, in 1936. So that the Keynesian proposal of full employment is definitely implemented, it is enough that the machines, as with supermarket cashiers, are occupied by more than one employee throughout the day: Each job should receive two employees a day, one in the morning and one in the afternoon, with companies receiving government incentives to maintain such a scheme. The government also has the role of qualifying the workforce and managing its placement in companies.

Under a policy of full employment, unemployment insurance and food stamps for healthy people are obsolete. Vocational high school becomes a matter of pure common sense, once the government has an obligation to provide the citizen with work, spending less if it does so earlier.

The main changes in society due to the advent of permanent full employment policy will be:

1) *Stability*. The figure of dismissal of employees is declared extinct, replaced by transfers, being government agencies responsible for receiving and requalifying, offering allowance, those who are not immediately rehired in the labor market.

2) *House*. Every head of household, male or female, is able to

take out a mortgage, so the problem of poor housing or homelessness disappears.

3) *Security*. The problem of crime is substantially reduced, by the lack of idle time among young people.

4) *Transport*. Traffic is greatly improved because of the distribution of working hours in less concentrated hours.

5) *Improvement*. The dispute for jobs becomes via better qualification, no longer because of the unemployed condition.

6) *Citizenship*. Greater respect is built up in the employer-employee relationship, as there are no desperate unemployed to fill the jobs on offer.

7) *Income*. There is an increase in the remuneration of the labor force, due to the absence of unemployed people, and, consequently, a considerable increase in GDP.

Unemployment has been, since 1936 (Keynes's book publication), a deliberate policy. War, until the end of Nazism (1945), was an unavoidable pathological policy, but from the knowledge we have accumulated in recent decades, it has become an option, for schizophrenic leaders and their doormats.

As for the direct election of the chief of State, the amount of damage to society caused by this practice, especially in the federal States, does not fit into a single book. Mania of Latin and Islamic countries until the beginning of the 21st century, with Turkey as a recent member of the sad club, the institution clearly shows that in the medium and long term it crystallizes poverty and throws the population into widespread mediocrity in every respect, cultural, artistic, sporting or scientific.

All these gains will be the fruit of the ultimate peace, which comes with the elimination of the three causes of war conflicts.

Myths. Is the "bloodbath" a necessity for progress?

For war to become a past story, it is necessary not only to recognize and disseminate the three causes, avoiding them at all costs, but also to undo, through education, harmful beliefs that have been cultivated over the centuries.

War has had two positive aspects throughout history. The first, Malthusian, was to slow the explosion of overpopulation before science developed birth control drugs. The second was that of pointing out among peoples in struggle which one or which ones presented technical superiority. This is because a war was hardly won by chance.

Excellence in war is winning without battle, Sun Tzu wrote. This is not a myth, but a glimpse that war itself should be abolished from human relations as soon as possible. Much differently, Machiavelli recorded that "a war may be postponed, but never prevented". In spite of the Florentine's acute intelligence, his phrase reveals contempt for diplomacy, as well as a pessimistic view of the human possibilities of discovering etiologies. Machiavelli's statement is one of the myths that must be dispelled. This is the myth **A**.

The need for a "bloodbath" for a country to reach maturity and reach its stage of development is another myth advocated by fascists and warmongers. The United States went through many indigenous wars against Eurodescendants and still went through the Anglo-American War (1812), the Mexican-American War (1846) and the American Civil War (1861), and became a very rich country. Now the wars had their causes and were far from being a bloodshed project to "purify" the souls of citizens. Canada did not war against the natives and did not go through civil war, becoming a rich and developed country. With a tradition of neutrality there is also Switzerland, a very rich country. On the contrary, North Korea suffered the most violent war in history in the early 1950s, and is one of the poorest countries in the world. Several other peoples who have suffered many wars remain poor and with no prospect of progress. The "bloodbath" as purification is the myth **B**.

There is also a very harmful myth linked to Islam. It is the interpretation that the Arabic word *jihad* means "holy war". The term, according to Arab philologists, means "effort" and is used in the sense of commitment by religion. Understanding it outside and within the Islamic world as "war for religion" or "holy war" is to play the game of human puppeteers. This is myth **C**.

However, the most damaging myth about war arose shortly after 1945 and accounts for the biased interpretation that the "war effort" was responsible for the full employment of 1944 in the United States. It's the myth **D**. Maybe the creators of this myth just came up with an explanation for what they didn't understand. The fact is that Keynesian economist John Kenneth Galbraith, Treasury Secretary, had two years earlier implemented a price freeze plan and tamed inflation, in addition to adopting policies proposed by Keynes, i. e., policies aimed at full employment.

Old-time. Is physical violence an adult trait?

Arrangements to eliminate these myths are a necessity because humanity has an unhealthy attachment to the past, not as a mere memory, but as an idyllic model. Slave labor was abolished worldwide in 1981, in Mauritania, but many insist on continuing to call slave labor what should be treated as servile labor, once slave labor comprises a type of employment relationship in which the contractor is officially the owner of the worker, something that can no longer exist. Other misfortunes of the human past that have been completely buried are considered still in force by large numbers of people.

Because of this veneration of the institutions of the past, the Islamic theocracy seized Tehran in 1979, restoring the stoning of adulterous women, forcing women to cover their heads with thick veils, executing homosexual men, and inspiring fanatical groups worldwide to commit terrorist acts. The Shiite wing of Islam, which set up the self-proclaimed "Iranian revolution", pushed the Sunni wing to try to overcome it by reactivating barbaric customs in the name of religion.

In order to prevent a romantic, past ruler from wishing to relive the war after it is wiped off the face of the Earth, a mechanism must be adopted at the UN, approved by the vast majority of member States: the chief of State - or government - who declares war to another country loses office the next day.

Physical violence is a childish trait, once it is in children that physical aggression hurts. Those who use physical violence in adulthood are those who grew up in body, but not in mind. Since war is the ultimate violence, an agent who reactivates it must be seen by his commanders as an individual with stunted brain, and should not count on their obedience or respect, except as a patient to be treated in the hospital bed. .

Collateral. Is there room for free and unlimited human reproduction?

The full employment regime and the establishment of anti-war fire doors have a collateral effect that requires comprehensive measures. As we had already eliminated our larger predators with armaments, and, since the twentieth century, lethal microorganisms, with antibiotics, we are moving to establish ourselves as, if not the only, at least the most harmful plague on the planet.

The only way to reverse the fate of being a plague is birth control, not just as a campaign but as an effective policy. Without this, we will not curb the rise of the anthropogenic global warming, nor will we enjoy for a long time the splendid benefit of the combination of full employment and peace. If the world's population expands much beyond the eight billion that we have in the end of the second decade of this millennium, there may even be food available, but problems with water, flora and climate will be greatly aggravated. The destruction of life on Earth can occur inexorably, as warned by Stephen Hawking, who believed that humanity had already passed the point of no return, given the damage done so far.

Regardless of how much time we have to live on the planet, it is necessary to teach children and adolescents to always avoid, aware of the dangers involved, these three irresponsibilities:

A) overpopulation;

B) long-lived ruler;

C) exception regime.

In any case, relying on human ingenuity to solve its great problems, especially those created by humanity itself, we must continue to struggle to leave behind us the era of unemployment and war.

Army. Is it up to the army to fight the war?

Three categories of public agents work as society's entourage scouts: Politicians, soldiers, and diplomats. They are the people who occupy the front line in one country's relations with another. Other civil servants and civil society form the rear.

With the abolition of war, the army and other military corps that have always been trained for defense will have to change their focus.

Certainly defense training cannot be abandoned at all, because the possibility of a war resurgence by one or another country can never be ruled out. The army must continue training.

But this is very little for a professional category that for millennia has been preparing almost exclusively to make war. Just as dentists are already adapting their activities to the imminent day when tooth decay can be avoided, by engaging in orthodontics and other actions, so the military must become accustomed to training for activities unrelated to war.

An open field for the military is the cause of sustainable development. The military can continue to help build public works such as hospitals, roads, waterways and bridges, but they need to be imbued with the spirit of sustainability. Taking responsibility for the environment is probably the healthiest attitude that can be embraced by armies in the third millennium.

The defense of borders to curb the action of looters and traffickers needs to be grounded in zeal for the environmental issue. The army, in addition to the duties already devoted to it in peacetime, is also responsible for replanting forests and restoring watercourses.

Another field that is already part of the army's performance and deserves more attention is the training of young people, civil and military, for Olympic sports. Konrad Lorenz, 1973 Nobel Prize winner in medicine, proposed replacing war with sports competition. Once the war abolition mechanism is consolidated and disseminated, the armed forces of the various countries will be on firm ground if among their concerns is this one of preparing athletes for disputes in various sports.

In the postwar times, the weapons used by the military must be stun guns (taser). Police must replace every deadly pistol with a taser, so that delinquents have strangled access to firearms. The more these lethal weapons are made for the military, police, and the so-called "good citizens", the more they reach the bandits.

Finally, the main role of the army should be the central role of preventing the three causes of war in each country, with the UN and its Peace Forces fulfilling the same mandate at the supranational level. If a President of the Republic pleads to extend the post beyond reasonable time, up to a maximum of 10 years, for example, it is up to the military, if civilians do not have the courage to do so, to remove the demented temptation from the chief of State, as the Zimbabwean generals did in November 2017, incidentally, in this case, with an unfortunate delay of several years - a premier can be tolerated for a maximum of four quadrennial terms, but ideally this limit should be set. in three quadrennia, especially if the regime is monarchical.

For a president, the ideal maximum term of office is four years without immediate or subsequent reelection. If the chief of State works to repeal the State-religion separation, for the purpose of establishing theocratic rule, the military must prevent him, when civilians are unable to do so. And if the chief of State decides to leave the capital with secular status in favor of residence in any other city in the country, it is up to the military, if the civilians are enchanted by that stupidity, to intercept the voyage of the energum. Neither riots, such as in Berlin 1919, nor the destruction of buildings and bridges, such as in Budapest 1945, nor even epidemics, should serve as guarantee for the transfer of the chief of State's residence from a consolidated capital to another city without this condition, unless there is a union of countries, in which case the chief must become resident in the main capital. In all three situations, the military must act after all resources of pressure and persuasion have been exhausted, and, finally, the remedial measure, which is not characterized as a coup, must be reported immediately to the UN Security Council. The successor provided for by the Constitution must be sworn in on the same day, and if he uses pusilanimity in returning the position to the harmful chief, both must be removed from their positions. After all, no national effort represents tragedy greater than war.

@cacildo

Made in the USA
Middletown, DE
08 July 2022

68836289R00086